COMPLEX AND SIMPLIFIED FORMS OF CHINESE CHARACTERS

with

Conversion Tables

by

John Montanaro

FAR EASTERN PUBLICATIONS

YALE UNIVERSITY

NEW HAVEN, CONNECTICUT

INTRODUCTORY NOTE

The purpose of making this compact little book available is to help the student of Chinese convert from one form of the character to the other, that is, from simplified to complex or complex to simplified. Most reference works now available will usually provide one form or the other, depending on where the work was published. Dictionaries published in China, with very few exceptions, will list only the simplified form, while dictionaries, reference works or textbooks produced in Taiwan (and sometimes Hong Kong) will provide the older, unsimplified form of the Chinese character. Hopefully this reference aid will be helpful to the student confronted by either form and needing to convert.

In addition to the conversion tables which form the main part of this book, a brief sketch of the character simplification movement has also been provided. Comments from readers are welcome.

John Montanaro
Yale University
1985

A Brief Note on the Simplified
Chinese Character

(The following brief historical sketch of reforms in the
written language of China does not seek to report new in-
formation but is rather a summation of available research
presented here for the convenience of students using this
conversion table.)

It was only after 1949, with the establishment of the
People's Republic, that most attention in the realm of
language reform was given to character simplification.
Previous to that time most reforms were concerned with
schemes for alphabetization. The motive for character
simplification, as expressed in many official pronounce-
ments, was that it was viewed as a means of achieving wider
literacy for the populace as a whole. It was also thought
that simplification would bring about more and more liter-
ate cadres at the lower levels of the Chinese bureaucracy.
Character simplification was regarded as one of the most
urgent tasks of the new state and one promoted from the
highest levels of government.

In June, 1950, the Chinese Ministry of Education
through the Committee on Language Reform, began work on
character simplification generally proceeding along two
lines: reduction in the total number of characters in
common use and reduction in the number of strokes used to
write Chinese characters. Some reduction in the sheer number of characters was achieved quickly with the publica-
tion of a list of about 1000 variant characters that were
to be eliminated from the language. This was helpful but,
since then, little else has been achieved in this direc-
tion. Most recently published Chinese-English character
dictionaries still list 6000 to 7000 individual characters
and most people believe that one needs to recognize around
3500 to 4000 characters (and their common combinations)
to be able to read Chinese fluently.

In contrast, reduction in the number of strokes of
individual characters, which is really the meaning of the
term 'simplification', has been carried out with considerable success. The historical facts are simple and
easily summarized: In 1956 the Committee on Language
Reform, with government approval, promulgated a list of

1

515 simplified characters and 54 simplified character components or parts of characters from which further simplifications were to be made in the future. Since many of these now officially simplified forms had been informally used already (around 300 of the 515) there was little opposition to this first attempt at reform. Characters simplified via this list were now indeed easier to write. A comparison of the simplified forms with their original unsimplified counterparts shows an average reduction from sixteen to eight strokes per single character. A further step was taken in 1964 when the Committee published a list of over two thousand simplified characters, many of which resulted from the application of the 54 simplified components. (This is the list given in this book). In that same year the Committee published a list of over 6000 standard characters for the use of printing houses in an attempt at standardization, a most welcome move. The traditional 214 radicals used for dictionary arrangement for centuries, were also affected by the simplification effort since many of the more complicated radicals were simplified while others were standardized and still others eliminated. The total number of radicals in most Chinese dictionaries now has settled to around 189.*

Alongside these moves at simplification and standardization, the Chinese made significant improvements in the related fields of lexicography and dictionary compilation, especially in English to Chinese technical dictionaries.

In 1977, during the Cultural Revolution, further attempts at character simplification were made but met with stiff opposition. In this stage, newly simplified forms were not simply popularly used but hitherto unofficial forms, but rather completely new characters, some generated by the masses and some created by professionals in various fields. Resistance had to do not only with the form of the newly coined characters but was also bound up with the view that the reform had gone quite far enough and further simplification would cause confusion. In the end the newly simplified forms were quietly withdrawn and are now undergoing further study.** It now appears that chances for additional simplifications seem thankfully remote, at least for the time being. Of course, other aspects of overall language reform in

*For more on radicals see page 8 .
** For some examples see page 14.

China, such as the popularization of putonghua and the use
of the now official transcription system, hanyu pinyin,
continue apace.

There is no question but that the simplified forms,
in use now for nearly thirty years, are universally ac-
cepted in China. Virtually all new publications are
printed in simplified characters. Of course, the old,
traditional forms are still visable in China on shop signs
or product labels, for example, and in some publications,
such as historical texts, wherein use of the old forms is
necessary. Moreover, quite recently, Peking has shown an
increased awareness of the problems which simplified characters have caused to the Chinese reading public outside
of China. For example, some dictionaries will list both
forms, old and new, textbooks produced in China but aimed
at the foreign learner, at least give lip service to the
old form, and starting in July, 1985, a special edition of
the People's Daily will be available completely in traditional characters. These efforts, however, are aimed at
the foreign consumer of Chinese. In China, of course,
schools teach the simplified forms exclusively and Chinese
who wish to read widely and quickly materials printed in
traditional characters would likely need special training
or at least considerable extra effort.

Some will wish to ask if the reform has been success-
ful. Any answer will need to consider the motives and
goals behind the reform effort. The ultimate goal was to
promote literacy. The idea was simple: the old, traditional characters composed of many strokes, were hard to
write. Reform the script by reducing the average amount
of strokes and characters will be easier to write. With
the burden of writing eased the job of learning to read
should proceed faster. Literacy rates will go up; China
will prosper. Sounds very attractive and perhaps there
have been some advances in literacy in China over the past
generation. But the extent to which simplification has
made Chinese easier to learn is very difficult to determine
accurately because at the same time that the simplification
process has been going on, China has, despite the ravages
of the Cultural Revolution, steadily improved its educa-
tional system to the point of near universal, lower level
education. Living conditions have also improved dramat-
ically, especially in the last five years. So if

literacy rates have gone up, can we credit character simplification as a significant factor? Even a preliminary
answer must await research.

How has the reform, if we can term it that, affected
those who study Chinese as a second language? It has, of
course, made the language even more difficult. Now there
are two forms of the same character to learn. Foreigners
studying Chinese, unlike native Chinese who only learn
the simplified form, usually will want to learn both forms
in order that he may be able to read publications from
China and also materials from Taiwan and Hong Kong where
the old forms still prevail. And naturally one needs to
recognize the old forms if one is to read anything produced in China before the era of reform. The divided
language has made life tougher for the student of Chinese.
But the clock cannot and will not be turned back. This
added difficulty is another obstacle we students of the
language must overcome. It is hoped that this slim
volume will make the task a bit easier.

Some Principles of the Simplifying Process

Listed below, in order of general importance, are some of
the principles that have guided the simplification process
both in the past times and during recent efforts.

1. to adopt as standard:
   commonly used, existing, simplified forms

辦 頭 對

办 头 对

simpler, antiquated or variant forms, still in current
use

個 萬 禮

个 万 礼

2. to adopt commonly used, simpler, "Grass Style" forms to replace complex forms. For printing purposes, the curved strokes of the "Grass Style" were altered into straight lines.

發 東 樂

发 东 乐

3. to simplify characters by:
   deleting redundant parts:

蟲

虫

making part of a complex character stand for the entire character (parts could be top, bottom, left side, right

聲 嚮 號

声 向 号

side, top and bottom, inner part, or outer frame).

條　　奮　　開　　廣

条　　奋　　开　　广

4. to use certain antiquated forms which also constitute components of present unsimplified forms, e.g.

complex form: 與 處 雲 電 貌 鬍 鬚

simplified form: 与 处 云 电 皃 胡 須

5. to use simpler characters as substitutes for complex characters having identical or similar sounds, e.g.

complex form: 圓 衹 穀 裏 蠶 薑 黨

simplified form: 元 只 谷 里 迭 姜 党

6. to use certain symbols to represent various components of complicated characters, for example:

又 is substituted for:

　　1. 雚 as in 欢 （歡）

　　2. 虘 as in 戏 （戲）

　　3. 對 as in 对 （對）

不 is substituted for:

　　1. 睘 as in 还 （還）

　　2. 褱 as in 坏 （壞）

　　　　 as in 怀 （懷）

舌　is substituted for:

　　1. 𤔔　as in 乱（亂）
　　　　　as in 辞（辭）
　　2. 商　as in 敌（敵）
　　　　　as in 适（適）

ⅥⅥⅤ　is substituted for:

　　1. 同　as in 兴（興）
　　2. 𡰪　as in 学（學）
　　　　　as in 觉（覺）
　　3. 𦥑　as in 誉（譽）
　　　　　as in 举（舉）
　　4. 隹　as in 应（應）
　　5. 刀　as in 𤼵（留）

7. Through the application of certain principles of character formation, to reconstruct Chinese characters:

   a. apply the principle of 'Logical Combination' wherein two graphs representing 'ideas' are combined in one character:

   complex form: 雙 滅 體 竈 陰 陽 寶

   simplified form: 双 灭 体 灶 阴 阳 宝

   b. apply the principle of 'Phonetic Compound' wherein one part of the character is connected with meaning and the other related to sound:

   complex form: 藝 優 機 燈 墳 擬 擔

   simplified form: 艺 优 机 灯 坟 拟 担

Simplification of Radicals

Gone are the days when the student of Chinese could open virtually any character dictionary and find the familiar list of 214 traditional radicals. The simplification process has affected the shape and stroke count of the radicals. The following brief analysis will attempt to sketch some of these changes:

1. First of all, the number of radicals listed in a particular dictionary will vary depending on the scope of the dictionary. Larger, more comprehensive dictionaries, which need to categorize many more characters, will list slightly more radicals. Smaller dictionaries, fewer radicals. One of the first tasks

of the student is to become very familiar
with the radical list of the dictionary
being used since success in locating a character in a dictionary so very often depends
on identification of the radical. THE PINYIN
CHINESE-ENGLISH DICTIONARY, edited by Pro-
fessor Wu Jingrong of the Beijing Foreign
Languages Institute, which has been fairly
well received, lists 227 separate categories
of radicals arranged by total stroke count.
Here are some ways in which the number of
radicals has increased:

a. radicals which in traditional lists had
   more than one form but were not separately
   listed are now listed as separate radicals
   on the principle that if the shape differs
   then that shape deserves its own place on
   the list. The application of this principle
   yields about ten additional listings.
   Here are some examples:

The forms on the right are now listed separately by stroke count. This more rational arrangement is helpful as long as the student realizes that 水 and 氵 represent the same meaning, "water," but are differently shaped.

b. many complicated radicals have been simplified into less complex forms:
Examples: (numbers preceding or following the character indicate total stroke count)

16.	龍	龙	5.
15.	齒	齿	8.
14.	齊	齐	6.
11.	鳥	鸟	5.
10.	馬	马	3.
7.	見	见	4.
11.	魚	鱼	8.
9.	風	风	4.
9.	頁	页	6.
8.	門	门	3.
7.	車	车	4.
7.	貝	贝	4.
18.	龜	龟	7.

The complex forms in the above examples have disappeared from the usual lists of radicals found in modern (mainland) Chinese dictionaries while in the following both forms, old and new, complex and simplified have been retained, yielding a few more forms.

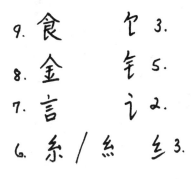

9. 食　　饣 3.

8. 金　　钅 5.

7. 言　　讠 2.

6. 系 / 糸　　纟 3.

Some radicals have simply been eliminated. Examples:

行

肉

長

Characters formerly grouped under these radicals are now listed differently. For example, 行 group characters are now listed under 彳 while those for 肉 are arranged under  .

Some completely new radicals have been devised
in order to accommodate changes in the script
and also because of regrouping of characters.
Example: 去 (qù) used to be classed under 厶 .
Now 去 is a new radical in itself.

業 (yè) is now simplified into 业 .
The latter is now a new radical accommo-
dating 业 and several other characters of
similar shape. 業 used to be classed under
the radical for wood 木 .

由 (yóu) used to be classed under
田 . 由 is now a radical by itself.
Other new radicals include:

申 　 戈
亦 　 冖
光 　 刁
是 　 ナ
亚 　 乂
尚 　 マ
　 　 乛

A special category called "Miscellaneous
Forms" has been created as the final listed
"radical" to accommodate about a dozen or so
characters which now do not fit into any
radical group.

And finally, another change which affects the
shapes and stroke count of radicals, concerns
the standardization of certain printed forms
of radicals. Here's some examples.

The forms on the right are now standardized
and appear as radicals. Hitherto they have
existed as alternate forms, variants or common
hand-written equivalents. The "older" forms
(on the left) are no longer used. Standardi-
zations like these are usually welcome news to
students. However, the usual caution must be
exercised because the older or non-standard
forms still appear in older texts or materials
or reference works produced in Taiwan or Hong
Kong.

Some examples of further simplified forms withdrawn during the third stage of character simplification:

芽 for 菜

宀 for 家

亍 for 街

劝 for 助

仈 for 儒

邦 for 帮

For those who wish to learn more about the reform the following list of books, while not definitive, will likely be helpful:

CHINA'S LANGUAGE REFORMS, Tao-t'ai Hsia. Far Eastern Publications, Yale University, 1956. A good, general survey of the early period of reform.

LANGUAGE AND LINGUISTICS IN THE PEOPLE'S REPUBLIC OF CHINA, Winfred P. Lehmann, editor. University of Texas Press, Austin, 1975. Surveys the reform but also includes such special topics such as, the teaching of English in China, language pathology, minority languages and lexicography.

THE CHINESE LANGUAGE: Fact and Fantasy, John DeFrancis. University of Hawaii Press, Honolulu, 1984. A wide-ranging, fascinating treatment of all aspects of modern Chinese.

COMPUTERS, LANGUAGE REFORM, AND LEXICOGRAPHY IN CHINA: A Report by the CETA Delegation, J. Mathias and T. Kennedy, eds. Pullman Press, Washington, 1980.

John Montanaro
Yale University, 1985

Guide to The Use of The Table

This book lists the official simplified forms now
in use in the People's Republic of China. These three
lists (A, B, and C) should provide students with the means
to find either the simplified form or the complex, traditional form of the character and also convert from one
to the other.

LIST "A" (page one) contains the simplified form on
the left and the complex form on the right in brackets
and is arranged in alphabetical order by hanyu pinyin
romanization.
Preceding this list is a conversion table containing the
three most common transcription systems: Wade-Giles,
Yale and hanyu pinyin.

LIST "B" (page 23) contains the same group of characters
as List A but is arranged by total stroke count of the
simplified character with the simplified form on the
left and the complex form on the right in brackets.

LIST "C" (page 42) arranges this same group according
to the total stroke count of the complex form enabling
the user to transfer from complex to simplified.

Characters having the same number of strokes on
Lists B or C are arranged according to the type of the
first stroke, that is, either heng (a horizontal stroke),
shu (a vertical stroke), pie (a stroke slanting down-
wards), dian (a dot), or zhe (an angular stroke, like
the corner of a square).
Examples: ─ │) ˋ ㄱ

Some simplified characters can also serve as simplified components of other more complex forms. Those
of this type are marked with an asterisk.

REMINDER: this booklet lists ONLY those characters
that have been effected by simplification. Characters
not so effected are not listed. This list of approxi-
mately 2200 characters is not at all a complete list of
Chinese characters in common use which, by the way,
number at least 6000. So if you look up a character and
do not find it on this list, it very likely means that
the character has not been simplified.

COMPARATIVE TRANSCRIPTION TABLE
Pinyin—Yale—Wade-Giles

Pinyin	Yale	Wade-Giles	Pinyin	Yale	Wade-Giles
a	a	a	ceng	tseng	ts'eng
ai	ai	ai	cha	cha	ch'a
an	an	an	chai	chai	ch'ai
ang	ang	ang	chan	chan	ch'an
ao	au	ao	chang	chang	ch'ang
			chao	chau	ch'ao
			che	che	ch'e
ba	ba	pa	chen	chen	ch'en
bai	bai	pai	cheng	cheng	ch'eng
ban	ban	pan	chi	chr	ch'ih
bang	bang	pang	chong	chung	ch'ung
bao	bau	pao	chou	chou	ch'ou
bei	bei	pei	chu	chu	ch'u
ben	ben	pen	chuai	chwai	ch'uai
beng	beng	peng	chuan	chwan	ch'uan
bi	bi	pi	chuang	chwang	ch'uang
bian	byan	pien	chui	chwei	ch'ui
biao	byau	piao	chun	chwun	ch'un
bie	bye	pieh	chuo	chwo	ch'o
bin	bin	pin	ci	tsz	tz'u
bing	bing	ping	cong	tsung	ts'ung
bo	bwo	po	cou	tsou	ts'ou
bou	bou	pou	cu	tsu	ts'u
bu	bu	pu	cuan	tswan	ts'uan
			cui	tswei	ts'ui
ca	tsa	ts'a	cun	tswun	ts'un
cai	tsai	ts'ai	cuo	tswo	ts'o
can	tsan	ts'an			
cang	tsang	ts'ang	da	da	ta
cao	tsao	ts'ao	dai	dai	tai
ce	tse	ts'e	dan	dan	tan
cen	tsen	ts'en			

17

Pinyin	Yale	Wade-Giles	Pinyin	Yale	Wade-Giles
dang	dang	tang	gai	gai	kai
dao	dau	tao	gan	gan	kan
de	de	te	gang	gang	kang
dei	dei	tei	gao	gau	kao
deng	deng	teng	ge	ge	ke, ko
di	di	ti	gei	gei	kei
dian	dyan	tien	gen	gen	ken
diao	dyau	tiao	geng	geng	keng
die	dye	tieh	gong	gung	kung
ding	ding	ting	gou	gou	kou
diu	dyou	tiu	gu	gu	ku
dong	dung	tung	gua	gwa	kua
dou	dou	tou	guai	gwai	kuai
du	du	tu	guan	gwan	kuan
duan	dwan	tuan	guang	gwang	kuang
dui	dwei	tui	gui	gwei	kuei
dun	dwun	tun	gun	gwun	kun
duo	dwo	to	guo	gwo	kuo
e	e	e, o	ha	ha	ha
ei	ei	ei	hai	hai	hai
en	en	en	han	han	han
eng	eng	eng	hang	hang	hang
er	er	erh	hao	hau	hao
			he	he	he, ho
fa	fa	fa	hei	hei	hei
fan	fan	fan	hen	hen	hen
fang	fang	fang	heng	heng	heng
fei	fei	fei	hong	hung	hung
fen	fen	fen	hou	hou	hou
feng	feng	feng	hu	hu	hu
fo	fwo	fo	hua	hwa	hua
fou	fou	fou	huai	hwai	huai
fu	fu	fu	huan	hwan	huan
			huang	hwang	huang
ga	ga	ka	hui	hwei	hui

Pinyin	Yale	Wade-Giles	Pinyin	Yale	Wade-Giles
hun	hwun	hun	la	la	la
huo	hwo	huo	lai	lai	lai
			lan	lan	lan
ji	ji	chi	lang	lang	lang
jia	jya	chia	lao	lau	lao
jian	jyan	chien	le	le	le
jiang	jyang	chiang	lei	lei	lei
jiao	jyau	chiao	leng	leng	leng
jie	jye	chieh	li	li	li
jin	jin	chin	lia	lya	lia
jing	jing	ching	lian	lyan	lien
jiong	jyong	chiung	liang	lyang	liang
jiu	jyou	chiu	liao	lyau	liao
ju	jyu	chü	lie	lye	lieh
juan	jywan	chüan	lin	lin	lin
jue	jywe	chüeh	ling	ling	ling
jun	jyun	chün	liu	lyou	liu
			long	lung	lung
ka	ka	k'a	lou	lou	lou
kai	kai	k'ai	lu	lu	lu
kan	kan	k'an	luan	lwan	luan
kang	kang	k'ang	lun	lwun	lun
kao	kau	k'ao	luo	lwo	lo
ke	ke	k'e, k'o	lü	lyu	lü
ken	ken	k'en	lüe	lywe	lüeh
keng	keng	k'eng			
kong	kung	k'ung	ma	ma	ma
kou	kou	k'ou	mai	mai	mai
ku	ku	k'u	man	man	man
kua	kwa	k'ua	mang	mang	mang
kuai	kwai	k'uai	mao	mau	mao
kuan	kwan	k'uan	mei	mei	mei
kuang	kwang	k'uang	men	men	men
kui	kwei	k'uei	meng	meng	meng
kun	kwen	k'un	mi	mi	mi
kuo	kwo	k'uo	mian	myan	mien

Pinyin	Yale	Wade-Giles	Pinyin	Yale	Wade-Giles
miao	myau	miao	pan	pan	p'an
mie	mye	mieh	pang	pang	p'ang
min	min	min	pao	pau	p'ao
ming	ming	ming	pei	pei	p'ei
miu	myou	miu	pen	pen	p'en
mo	mwo	mo	peng	peng	p'eng
mou	mou	mou	po	pwo	p'o
mu	mu	mu	pou	pou	p'ou
			pi	pi	p'i
			pian	pyan	p'ien
na	na	na	piao	pyau	p'iao
nai	nai	nai	pie	pye	p'ieh
nan	nan	nan	pin	pin	p'in
nang	nang	nang	ping	ping	p'ing
nao	nau	nao	pu	pu	p'u
ne	ne	ne			
nei	nei	nei	qi	chi	ch'i
nen	nen	nen	qia	chya	ch'ia
neng	neng	neng	qian	chyan	ch'ien
nong	nung	nung	qiang	chyang	ch'iang
nou	nou	nou	qiao	chyau	ch'iao
ni	ni	ni	qie	chye	ch'ieh
nian	nyan	nien	qin	chin	ch'in
niang	nyang	niang	qing	ching	ch'ing
niao	nyau	niao	qiong	chyung	ch'iung
nie	nye	nieh	qiu	chyou	ch'iu
nin	nin	nin	qu	chyu	ch'ü
ning	ning	ning	quan	chywan	ch'üan
niu	nyou	niu	que	chywe	ch'üeh
nu	nu	nu	qun	chyun	ch'ün
nuan	nwan	nuan			
nuo	nwo	no	ran	ran	jan
nü	nyu	nü	rang	rang	jang
nüe	nywe	nüeh	rao	rau	jao
			re	re	je
pa	pa	p'a	ren	ren	jen
pai	pai	p'ai			

Pinyin	Yale	Wade-Giles	Pinyin	Yale	Wade-Giles
reng	reng	jeng	shuo	shwo	shuo
ri	r	jih	si	sz	szu
rong	rung	jung	song	sung	sung
rou	rou	jou	sou	sou	sou
ru	ru	ju	su	su	su
ruan	rwan	juan	suan	swan	suan
rui	rwei	jui	sui	swei	sui
run	rwen	jun	sun	swun	sun
ruo	rwo	jo	suo	swo	so
sa	sa	sa	ta	ta	t'a
sai	sai	sai	tai	tai	t'ai
san	san	san	tan	tan	t'an
sang	sang	sang	tang	tang	t'ang
sao	sau	sao	tao	tau	t'ao
se	se	se	te	te	t'e
sen	sen	sen	teng	teng	t'eng
seng	seng	seng	ti	ti	t'i
sha	sha	sha	tian	tyan	t'ien
shai	shai	shai	tiao	tyau	t'iao
shan	shan	shan	tie	tye	t'ieh
shang	shang	shang	ting	ting	t'ing
shao	shau	shao	tong	tung	t'ung
she	she	she	tou	tou	t'ou
shei	shei	shei	tu	tu	t'u
shen	shen	shen	tuan	twan	t'uan
sheng	sheng	sheng	tui	twei	t'ui
shi	shr	shih	tun	twun	t'un
shou	shou	shou	tuo	two	t'o
shu	shu	shu			
shua	shwa	shua	wa	wa	wa
shuai	shwai	shuai	wai	wai	wai
shuan	shwan	shuan	wan	wan	wan
shuang	shwang	shuang	wang	wang	wang
shui	shwei	shui	wei	wei	wei
shun	shwen	shun	wen	wen	wen

Pinyin	Yale	Wade-Giles	Pinyin	Yale	Wade-Giles
weng	weng	weng	zan	dzan	tsan
wo	wo	wo	zang	dzang	tsang
wu	wu	wu	zao	dzau	tsao
			ze	dze	tse
xi	syi	hsi	zei	dzei	tsei
xia	sya	hsia	zen	dzen	tsen
xian	syan	hsien	zeng	dzeng	tseng
xiang	syang	hsiang	zha	ja	cha
xiao	syau	hsiao	zhai	jai	chai
xie	sye	hsieh	zhan	jan	chan
xin	syin	hsin	zhang	jang	chang
xing	sying	hsing	zhao	jau	chao
xiong	syung	hsiung	zhe	je	che
xiu	syou	hsiu	zhei	jei	chei
xu	syu	hsü	zhen	jen	chen
xuan	sywan	hsüan	zheng	jeng	cheng
xue	sywe	hsüeh	zhi	jr	chih
xun	syun	hsün	zhong	jung	chung
			zhou	jou	chou
ya	ya	ya	zhu	ju	chu
yan	yan	yen	zhua	jwa	chua
yang	yang	yang	zhuai	jwai	chuai
yao	yau	yao	zhuan	jwan	chuan
ye	ye	yeh	zhuang	jwang	chuang
yi	yi	i	zhui	jwei	chui
yin	yin	yin	zhun	jwun	chun
ying	ying	ying	zhuo	jwo	cho
yong	yung	yung	zi	dz	tzu
you	you	yu	zong	dzung	tsung
yu	yu	yü	zou	dzou	tsou
yuan	ywan	yüan	zu	dzu	tsu
yue	ywe	yüeh	zuan	dzwan	tsuan
yun	yun	yün	zui	dzwei	tsui
			zun	dzwen	tsun
za	dza	tsa	zuo	dzwo	tso
zai	dzai	tsai			

Conversion Table of Complex and Simplified Forms of Chinese Characters

繁 简 字 对 照 表

✱ = See page 15 note

Hanyu Pinyin to Simplified / Complex Form

A. 从拼音查汉字

A

a

锕〔錒〕

ai

锿〔鎄〕
皑〔皚〕
霭〔靄〕
蔼〔藹〕
*爱〔愛〕
嗳〔嚘〕
瑷〔璦〕
嗳〔噯〕
暧〔曖〕
媛〔嬡〕
碍〔礙〕

an

谙〔諳〕
鹌〔鵪〕
铵〔銨〕

ang

肮〔骯〕

ao

鳌〔鰲〕
骜〔驁〕
袄〔襖〕

B

ba

鲅〔鮁〕
钯〔鈀〕
坝〔壩〕
*罢〔罷〕
耙〔糤〕

bai

摆〔擺〕
〔襬〕
败〔敗〕

ban

颁〔頒〕
板〔闆〕
绊〔絆〕
办〔辦〕

bang

帮〔幫〕
绑〔綁〕
谤〔謗〕
镑〔鎊〕

bao

龅〔齙〕
宝〔寶〕
饱〔飽〕
鸨〔鴇〕
报〔報〕
鲍〔鮑〕

bei

惫〔憊〕
辈〔輩〕
*贝〔貝〕
钡〔鋇〕
狈〔狽〕
*备〔備〕
呗〔唄〕

ben

锛〔錛〕
贲〔賁〕

beng

绷〔繃〕
镚〔鏰〕

bi

*笔〔筆〕
铋〔鉍〕
贲〔賁〕
*毕〔畢〕
哔〔嗶〕
筚〔篳〕
荜〔蓽〕
跸〔蹕〕
滗〔潷〕
币〔幣〕
闭〔閉〕
毙〔斃〕

bian

鳊〔鯿〕
编〔編〕
*边〔邊〕
笾〔籩〕
贬〔貶〕
辩〔辯〕
辫〔辮〕
变〔變〕

biao

镳〔鑣〕
标〔標〕
骠〔驃〕

1

镖〔鏢〕
飙〔飆〕
表〔錶〕
鳔〔鰾〕
bie
鳖〔鱉〕
瘪〔癟〕
别〔彆〕
bin
*宾〔賓〕
滨〔濱〕
槟〔檳〕
傧〔儐〕
缤〔繽〕
镔〔鑌〕
濒〔瀕〕
鬓〔鬢〕
摈〔擯〕
殡〔殯〕
膑〔臏〕
髌〔髕〕
bing
槟〔檳〕
饼〔餅〕
bo
饽〔餑〕

钵〔鉢〕
拨〔撥〕
鹁〔鵓〕
馎〔餺〕
钹〔鈸〕
驳〔駁〕
铂〔鉑〕
卜〔蔔〕
bu
补〔補〕
钚〔鈈〕

C

cai
才〔纔〕
财〔財〕
can
*参〔參〕
骖〔驂〕
蚕〔蠶〕
惭〔慚〕
残〔殘〕
惨〔慘〕
穇〔穇〕
灿〔燦〕

cang
*仓〔倉〕
沧〔滄〕
苍〔蒼〕
伧〔傖〕
鸧〔鶬〕
舱〔艙〕
ce
测〔測〕
恻〔惻〕
厕〔厠〕
侧〔側〕
cen
*参〔參〕
ceng
层〔層〕
cha
馇〔餷〕
锸〔鍤〕
镲〔鑔〕
诧〔詫〕
chai
钗〔釵〕
侪〔儕〕
虿〔蠆〕

chan
搀〔攙〕
掺〔摻〕
缠〔纏〕
禅〔禪〕
蝉〔蟬〕
婵〔嬋〕
谗〔讒〕
馋〔饞〕
*产〔産〕
浐〔滻〕
铲〔鏟〕
蒇〔蕆〕
阐〔闡〕
辗〔輾〕
谄〔諂〕
颤〔顫〕
忏〔懺〕
划〔剗〕
chang
伥〔倀〕
阊〔閶〕
鲳〔鯧〕
*尝〔嘗〕
偿〔償〕
鲿〔鱨〕

*长〔長〕
肠〔腸〕
场〔場〕
厂〔廠〕
怅〔悵〕
畅〔暢〕
chao
钞〔鈔〕
che
*车〔車〕
砗〔硨〕
彻〔徹〕
chen
谌〔諶〕
尘〔塵〕
陈〔陳〕
碜〔磣〕
榇〔櫬〕
衬〔襯〕
谶〔讖〕
称〔稱〕
龀〔齔〕
cheng
柽〔檉〕
蛏〔蟶〕

2

铛〔鐺〕
赪〔赬〕
称〔稱〕
枨〔棖〕
诚〔誠〕
惩〔懲〕
骋〔騁〕

chi

鸱〔鴟〕
迟〔遲〕
驰〔馳〕
*齿〔齒〕
炽〔熾〕
饬〔飭〕

chong

冲〔衝〕
*虫〔蟲〕
宠〔寵〕
铳〔銃〕

chou

绸〔紬〕
畴〔疇〕
筹〔籌〕
踌〔躊〕
俦〔儔〕
雠〔讎〕

绸〔綢〕
丑〔醜〕

chu

出〔齣〕
锄〔鋤〕
*刍〔芻〕
雏〔雛〕
储〔儲〕
础〔礎〕
处〔處〕
绌〔絀〕
触〔觸〕

chuai

闯〔闖〕

chuan

传〔傳〕
钏〔釧〕

chuang

疮〔瘡〕
闯〔闖〕
怆〔愴〕
创〔創〕

chui

锤〔錘〕

chun

鲼〔鰆〕

鹑〔鶉〕
纯〔純〕
莼〔蒓〕

chuo

绰〔綽〕
龊〔齪〕
辍〔輟〕

ci

鹚〔鷀〕
辞〔辭〕
词〔詞〕
赐〔賜〕

cong

聪〔聰〕
骢〔驄〕
枞〔樅〕
苁〔蓯〕
*从〔從〕
丛〔叢〕

cou

辏〔輳〕

cuan

撺〔攛〕
蹿〔躥〕
镩〔鑹〕
攒〔攢〕

*窜〔竄〕

cui

缞〔縗〕

cuo

嵯〔鹺〕
错〔錯〕
锉〔銼〕

D

da

*达〔達〕
哒〔噠〕
鞑〔韃〕

dai

贷〔貸〕
绐〔紿〕
*带〔帶〕
叇〔靆〕

dan

*单〔單〕
担〔擔〕
殚〔殫〕
箪〔簞〕
郸〔鄲〕
掸〔撣〕
胆〔膽〕

赕〔賧〕
惮〔憚〕
瘅〔癉〕
弹〔彈〕
诞〔誕〕

dang

裆〔襠〕
铛〔鐺〕
*当〔當〕
〔噹〕
*党〔黨〕
谠〔讜〕
挡〔擋〕
档〔檔〕
砀〔碭〕
荡〔蕩〕

dao

鱽〔魛〕
祷〔禱〕
岛〔島〕
捣〔搗〕
导〔導〕

de

锝〔鍀〕

deng

灯〔燈〕

3

镫〔鐙〕 钓〔釣〕 窦〔竇〕 顿〔頓〕 **er**
邓〔鄧〕 调〔調〕 **du** **duo** 儿〔兒〕
di **die** 读〔讀〕 夺〔奪〕 鸸〔鴯〕
镝〔鏑〕 谍〔諜〕 渎〔瀆〕 铎〔鐸〕 饵〔餌〕
觌〔覿〕 鲽〔鰈〕 椟〔櫝〕 驮〔馱〕 铒〔鉺〕
籴〔糴〕 绖〔絰〕 牍〔牘〕 堕〔墮〕 *尔〔爾〕
敌〔敵〕 迭〔叠〕 犊〔犢〕 础〔础〕 迩〔邇〕
涤〔滌〕 **ding** 牍〔牘〕 贰〔貳〕
诋〔詆〕 钉〔釘〕 独〔獨〕 **E**
谛〔諦〕 顶〔頂〕 赌〔賭〕 **F**
缔〔締〕 订〔訂〕 笃〔篤〕 **e**
递〔遞〕 锭〔錠〕 镀〔鍍〕 额〔額〕 **fa**
dian **diu** **duan** 锇〔鋨〕 *发〔發〕
颠〔顛〕 铥〔銩〕 *断〔斷〕 鹅〔鵝〕 〔髪〕
癫〔癲〕 **dong** 锻〔鍛〕 讹〔訛〕 罚〔罰〕
巅〔巔〕 *东〔東〕 缎〔緞〕 恶〔惡〕 阀〔閥〕
点〔點〕 鸫〔鶇〕 簖〔籪〕 〔噁〕 **fan**
淀〔澱〕 岽〔崬〕 **dui** 垩〔堊〕 烦〔煩〕
垫〔墊〕 冬〔鼕〕 怼〔懟〕 轭〔軛〕 矾〔礬〕
电〔電〕 *动〔動〕 *对〔對〕 谔〔諤〕 钒〔釩〕
钿〔鈿〕 冻〔凍〕 *队〔隊〕 鹗〔鶚〕 贩〔販〕
diao 栋〔棟〕 **dun** 鳄〔鰐〕 饭〔飯〕
鲷〔鯛〕 胨〔腖〕 吨〔噸〕 锷〔鍔〕 范〔範〕
铫〔銚〕 **dou** 镦〔鐓〕 饿〔餓〕 **fang**
铞〔銱〕 斜〔鈄〕 蹾〔蔮〕 **ê** 钫〔鈁〕
窎〔窵〕 斗〔鬥〕 钝〔鈍〕 诶〔誒〕 鲂〔魴〕
访〔訪〕

4

纺〔紡〕

fei

绯〔緋〕
鲱〔鯡〕
飞〔飛〕
诽〔誹〕
废〔廢〕
费〔費〕
镄〔鐨〕

fen

纷〔紛〕
坟〔墳〕
豮〔豶〕
粪〔糞〕
愤〔憤〕
偾〔僨〕
奋〔奮〕

feng

*丰〔豐〕
沣〔灃〕
锋〔鋒〕
*风〔風〕
沨〔渢〕
疯〔瘋〕
枫〔楓〕
砜〔碸〕

冯〔馮〕
缝〔縫〕
讽〔諷〕
凤〔鳳〕
赗〔賵〕

fu

麸〔麩〕
肤〔膚〕
辐〔輻〕
韨〔韍〕
绂〔紱〕
凫〔鳧〕
绋〔紼〕
辅〔輔〕
抚〔撫〕
赋〔賦〕
赙〔賻〕
缚〔縛〕
讣〔訃〕
复〔復〕
　〔複〕
　〔覆〕
鲋〔鮒〕
驸〔駙〕
鲋〔鮒〕
负〔負〕

妇〔婦〕

G

ga

钆〔釓〕

gai

该〔該〕
赅〔賅〕
盖〔蓋〕
钙〔鈣〕

gan

干〔乾〕
　〔幹〕
尴〔尷〕
赶〔趕〕
赣〔贛〕
绀〔紺〕

gang

*冈〔岡〕
刚〔剛〕
枫〔棡〕
纲〔綱〕
钢〔鋼〕
掆〔摃〕
岗〔崗〕

gao

镐〔鎬〕
缟〔縞〕
诰〔誥〕
锆〔鋯〕

ge

鸽〔鴿〕
搁〔擱〕
镉〔鎘〕
颌〔頜〕
阁〔閣〕
个〔個〕
铬〔鉻〕

gei

给〔給〕

geng

赓〔賡〕
鹒〔鶊〕
鲠〔鯁〕
绠〔綆〕

gong

龚〔龔〕
巩〔鞏〕
贡〔貢〕
唝〔嗊〕

gou

缑〔緱〕
沟〔溝〕
钩〔鈎〕
觏〔覯〕
诟〔詬〕
构〔構〕
购〔購〕

gu

轱〔軲〕
鸪〔鴣〕
诂〔詁〕
钴〔鈷〕
贾〔賈〕
蛊〔蠱〕
毂〔轂〕
馉〔餶〕
鹘〔鶻〕
谷〔穀〕
鹄〔鵠〕
顾〔顧〕
锢〔錮〕

gua

刮〔颳〕
鸹〔鴰〕
剐〔剮〕

5

诖〔詿〕

guan

关〔關〕
纶〔綸〕
鳏〔鰥〕
观〔觀〕
馆〔館〕
鹳〔鸛〕
贯〔貫〕
惯〔慣〕
掼〔摜〕

guang

*广〔廣〕
犷〔獷〕

gui

妫〔媯〕
沩〔潙〕
规〔規〕
鲑〔鮭〕
闺〔閨〕
*归〔歸〕
*龟〔龜〕
轨〔軌〕
匦〔匭〕
诡〔詭〕
鳜〔鱖〕

柜〔櫃〕
贵〔貴〕
刿〔劌〕
桧〔檜〕
刽〔劊〕

gun

辊〔輥〕
绲〔緄〕
鲧〔鯀〕

guo

涡〔渦〕
埚〔堝〕
蝈〔蟈〕
*国〔國〕
掴〔摑〕
帼〔幗〕
馃〔餜〕
腘〔膕〕
*过〔過〕

H

ha

铪〔鉿〕

hai

还〔還〕

骇〔駭〕

han

顸〔頇〕
韩〔韓〕
阚〔闞〕
㘎〔㘚〕
汉〔漢〕
颔〔頷〕

hang

绗〔絎〕
颃〔頏〕

hao

颢〔顥〕
灏〔灝〕
号〔號〕

he

诃〔訶〕
阂〔閡〕
阖〔闔〕
鹖〔鶡〕
颌〔頜〕
饸〔餄〕
合〔閤〕
纥〔紇〕
鹤〔鶴〕
贺〔賀〕

吓〔嚇〕

heng

鸻〔鴴〕

hong

轰〔轟〕
黉〔黌〕
鸿〔鴻〕
红〔紅〕
荭〔葒〕
讧〔訌〕

hou

后〔後〕
鲎〔鱟〕

hu

轷〔軤〕
壶〔壺〕
胡〔鬍〕
鹕〔鶘〕
鹄〔鵠〕
鹘〔鶻〕
浒〔滸〕
沪〔滬〕
护〔護〕

hua

*华〔華〕
骅〔驊〕

哗〔嘩〕
铧〔鏵〕
*画〔畫〕
婳〔嫿〕
划〔劃〕
桦〔樺〕
话〔話〕

huai

怀〔懷〕
坏〔壞〕

huan

欢〔歡〕
还〔還〕
环〔環〕
缳〔繯〕
镮〔鐶〕
锾〔鍰〕
缓〔緩〕
鲩〔鯇〕

huang

鳇〔鰉〕
谎〔謊〕

hui

挥〔揮〕
辉〔輝〕
翚〔翬〕

6

诙〔詼〕　祸〔禍〕　虮〔蟣〕　郏〔郟〕　捡〔撿〕
回〔迴〕　货〔貨〕　济〔濟〕　贾〔賈〕　睑〔瞼〕
*汇〔匯〕　　　　霁〔霽〕　槚〔檟〕　俭〔儉〕
　〔彙〕　**J**　荠〔薺〕　钾〔鉀〕　裥〔襇〕
贿〔賄〕　**ji**　剂〔劑〕　价〔價〕　简〔簡〕
秽〔穢〕　　　　鲚〔鱭〕　驾〔駕〕　谏〔諫〕
*会〔會〕　齑〔齏〕　际〔際〕　**jian**　渐〔漸〕
烩〔燴〕　跻〔躋〕　绩〔績〕　鹣〔鶼〕　槛〔檻〕
荟〔薈〕　击〔擊〕　计〔計〕　鳒〔鰜〕　贱〔賤〕
绘〔繪〕　赍〔賫〕　系〔繫〕　缣〔縑〕　溅〔濺〕
海〔海〕　缉〔緝〕　骥〔驥〕　*戋〔戔〕　践〔踐〕
殨〔殨〕　积〔積〕　觊〔覬〕　笺〔箋〕　饯〔餞〕
讳〔諱〕　羁〔羈〕　蓟〔薊〕　坚〔堅〕　*荐〔薦〕
hun　机〔機〕　鲫〔鯽〕　鲣〔鰹〕　鉴〔鑒〕
荤〔葷〕　饥〔饑〕　记〔記〕　缄〔緘〕　*见〔見〕
阍〔閽〕　讥〔譏〕　纪〔紀〕　鞯〔韉〕　枧〔梘〕
浑〔渾〕　玑〔璣〕　继〔繼〕　*监〔監〕　舰〔艦〕
珲〔琿〕　矶〔磯〕　**jia**　歼〔殲〕　剑〔劍〕
馄〔餛〕　叽〔嘰〕　家〔傢〕　艰〔艱〕　键〔鍵〕
诨〔諢〕　鸡〔鷄〕　镓〔鎵〕　间〔間〕　涧〔澗〕
huo　鹡〔鶺〕　*夹〔夾〕　谫〔譾〕　锏〔鐧〕
钬〔鈥〕　辑〔輯〕　浃〔浹〕　硷〔鹻〕　**jiang**
伙〔夥〕　极〔極〕　颊〔頰〕　拣〔揀〕　姜〔薑〕
镬〔鑊〕　级〔級〕　荚〔莢〕　笕〔筧〕　*将〔將〕
获〔獲〕　挤〔擠〕　蛱〔蛺〕　茧〔繭〕　浆〔漿〕
　〔穫〕　给〔給〕　铗〔鋏〕　检〔檢〕　缰〔繮〕
　　　　*几〔幾〕

7

讲〔講〕

桨〔槳〕

奖〔獎〕

蒋〔蔣〕

酱〔醬〕

绛〔絳〕

jiao

胶〔膠〕

鲛〔鮫〕

鹪〔鷦〕

浇〔澆〕

骄〔驕〕

娇〔嬌〕

鹪〔鷦〕

饺〔餃〕

铰〔鉸〕

绞〔絞〕

侥〔僥〕

矫〔矯〕

搅〔攪〕

缴〔繳〕

觉〔覺〕

较〔較〕

轿〔轎〕

挢〔撟〕

峤〔嶠〕

jie

阶〔階〕

疖〔癤〕

讦〔訐〕

洁〔潔〕

诘〔詰〕

撷〔擷〕

颉〔頡〕

结〔結〕

鲒〔鮚〕

*节〔節〕

借〔藉〕

诫〔誡〕

jin

谨〔謹〕

馑〔饉〕

觐〔覲〕

紧〔緊〕

锦〔錦〕

仅〔僅〕

劲〔勁〕

*进〔進〕

琎〔璡〕

缙〔縉〕

*尽〔盡〕

〔儘〕

浕〔濜〕

荩〔藎〕

赆〔贐〕

烬〔燼〕

jing

惊〔驚〕

鲸〔鯨〕

鹒〔鶊〕

泾〔涇〕

茎〔莖〕

经〔經〕

颈〔頸〕

刭〔剄〕

镜〔鏡〕

竞〔競〕

痉〔痙〕

劲〔勁〕

胫〔脛〕

径〔徑〕

靓〔靚〕

jiu

纠〔糾〕

鸠〔鳩〕

阄〔鬮〕

鹫〔鷲〕

旧〔舊〕

ju

*车〔車〕

驹〔駒〕

鵙〔鶪〕

锔〔鋦〕

*举〔舉〕

龃〔齟〕

榉〔櫸〕

讵〔詎〕

惧〔懼〕

飓〔颶〕

窭〔窶〕

屦〔屨〕

据〔據〕

剧〔劇〕

锯〔鋸〕

juan

鹃〔鵑〕

镌〔鎸〕

卷〔捲〕

绢〔絹〕

jue

觉〔覺〕

镢〔钁〕

钁〔钁〕

谲〔譎〕

诀〔訣〕

绝〔絕〕

jun

军〔軍〕

皲〔皸〕

钧〔鈞〕

骏〔駿〕

K

kai

开〔開〕

锎〔鐦〕

恺〔愷〕

垲〔塏〕

剀〔剴〕

铠〔鎧〕

凯〔凱〕

闿〔闓〕

锴〔鍇〕

忾〔愾〕

kan

龛〔龕〕

槛〔檻〕

kang

钪〔鈧〕

8

kao

铐〔銬〕

ke

颏〔頦〕
轲〔軻〕
钶〔鈳〕
颗〔顆〕
*壳〔殼〕
缂〔緙〕
克〔剋〕
课〔課〕
骒〔騍〕
锞〔錁〕

ken

恳〔懇〕
垦〔墾〕

keng

铿〔鏗〕

kou

抠〔摳〕
眍〔瞘〕

ku

库〔庫〕
裤〔褲〕
绔〔絝〕
喾〔嚳〕

kua

夸〔誇〕

kuai

㧟〔擓〕
*会〔會〕
浍〔澮〕
哙〔噲〕
郐〔鄶〕
侩〔儈〕
脍〔膾〕
鲙〔鱠〕
狯〔獪〕
块〔塊〕

kuan

宽〔寬〕
髋〔髖〕

kuang

诓〔誆〕
诳〔誑〕
矿〔礦〕
圹〔壙〕
旷〔曠〕
纩〔纊〕
邝〔鄺〕
贶〔貺〕

kui

窥〔窺〕
亏〔虧〕
岿〔巋〕
溃〔潰〕
襁〔禬〕
愦〔憒〕
聩〔聵〕
匮〔匱〕
蒉〔蕢〕
馈〔饋〕
篑〔簣〕

kun

鲲〔鯤〕
锟〔錕〕
壸〔壼〕
阃〔閫〕
困〔睏〕

kuo

阔〔闊〕
扩〔擴〕

L

la

蜡〔蠟〕
腊〔臘〕

镴〔鑞〕

lai

*来〔來〕
徕〔倈〕
莱〔萊〕
崃〔崍〕
铼〔錸〕
徕〔徠〕
赖〔賴〕
濑〔瀨〕
癞〔癩〕
籁〔籟〕
睐〔睞〕
赍〔賚〕

lan

兰〔蘭〕
栏〔欄〕
拦〔攔〕
阑〔闌〕
澜〔瀾〕
谰〔讕〕
斓〔斕〕
镧〔鑭〕
褴〔襤〕
蓝〔藍〕
篮〔籃〕

岚〔嵐〕
懒〔懶〕
览〔覽〕
榄〔欖〕
揽〔攬〕
缆〔纜〕
烂〔爛〕
滥〔濫〕

lang

锒〔鋃〕
阆〔閬〕

lao

捞〔撈〕
劳〔勞〕
崂〔嶗〕
痨〔癆〕
铹〔鐒〕
铑〔銠〕
涝〔澇〕
唠〔嘮〕
耢〔耮〕

le

鳓〔鰳〕
*乐〔樂〕
饹〔餎〕

9

lei

镭〔鐳〕
累〔纍〕
缧〔縲〕
诔〔誄〕
垒〔壘〕
类〔類〕

li

*离〔離〕
漓〔灕〕
篱〔籬〕
缡〔縭〕
骊〔驪〕
鹂〔鸝〕
鲡〔鱺〕
礼〔禮〕
逦〔邐〕
里〔裏〕
锂〔鋰〕
鲤〔鯉〕
鳢〔鱧〕
*丽〔麗〕
俪〔儷〕
郦〔酈〕
厉〔厲〕
励〔勵〕

砾〔礫〕
*历〔歷〕
　〔曆〕
沥〔瀝〕
坜〔壢〕
疬〔癧〕
雳〔靂〕
枥〔櫪〕
苈〔藶〕
呖〔嚦〕
疠〔癘〕
栃〔櫔〕
砺〔礪〕
蛎〔蠣〕
栎〔櫟〕
轹〔轢〕
隶〔隸〕

lia

俩〔倆〕

lian

帘〔簾〕
镰〔鐮〕
联〔聯〕
连〔連〕
涟〔漣〕
莲〔蓮〕

鲢〔鰱〕
琏〔璉〕
奁〔奩〕
怜〔憐〕
敛〔斂〕
蔹〔蘞〕
脸〔臉〕
恋〔戀〕
链〔鏈〕
炼〔煉〕
练〔練〕
潋〔瀲〕
殓〔殮〕
裣〔襝〕
裢〔褳〕

liang

粮〔糧〕
*两〔兩〕
俩〔倆〕
唡〔啢〕
魉〔魎〕
谅〔諒〕
辆〔輛〕

liao

鹩〔鷯〕
缭〔繚〕

疗〔療〕
辽〔遼〕
了〔瞭〕
钌〔釕〕
镣〔鐐〕

lie

猎〔獵〕
鸦〔鴷〕

lin

辚〔轔〕
鳞〔鱗〕
临〔臨〕
邻〔鄰〕
蔺〔藺〕
躏〔躪〕
赁〔賃〕

ling

鲮〔鯪〕
绫〔綾〕
龄〔齡〕
铃〔鈴〕
鸰〔鴒〕
*灵〔靈〕
棂〔欞〕
领〔領〕

岭〔嶺〕

liu

飗〔飀〕
*刘〔劉〕
浏〔瀏〕
骝〔騮〕
镏〔鎦〕
绺〔綹〕
馏〔餾〕
鹨〔鷚〕
陆〔陸〕

long

*龙〔龍〕
泷〔瀧〕
珑〔瓏〕
聋〔聾〕
栊〔櫳〕
砻〔礱〕
笼〔籠〕
茏〔蘢〕
咙〔嚨〕
昽〔曨〕
胧〔朧〕
垄〔壟〕
拢〔攏〕
陇〔隴〕

10

lou
睽〔瞜〕
*娄〔婁〕
偻〔僂〕
喽〔嘍〕
楼〔樓〕
溇〔漊〕
蒌〔蔞〕
髅〔髏〕
蝼〔螻〕
耧〔耬〕
搂〔摟〕
嵝〔嶁〕
篓〔簍〕
瘘〔瘻〕
镂〔鏤〕
lu
噜〔嚕〕
庐〔廬〕
炉〔爐〕
芦〔蘆〕
*卢〔盧〕
泸〔瀘〕
垆〔壚〕
栌〔櫨〕
颅〔顱〕

鸬〔鸕〕
胪〔臚〕
鲈〔鱸〕
舻〔艫〕
*卤〔鹵〕
〔滷〕
*虏〔虜〕
掳〔擄〕
鲁〔魯〕
橹〔櫓〕
镥〔鑥〕
辘〔轆〕
辂〔輅〕
赂〔賂〕
鹭〔鷺〕
陆〔陸〕
*录〔錄〕
箓〔籙〕
绿〔綠〕
轳〔轤〕
氇〔氌〕
lü
驴〔驢〕
闾〔閭〕
榈〔櫚〕
屡〔屢〕

偻〔僂〕
褛〔褸〕
缕〔縷〕
铝〔鋁〕
*虑〔慮〕
滤〔濾〕
绿〔綠〕
luan
娈〔孌〕
栾〔欒〕
滦〔灤〕
峦〔巒〕
脔〔臠〕
銮〔鑾〕
挛〔攣〕
鸾〔鸞〕
孪〔孿〕
乱〔亂〕
lun
抡〔掄〕
*仑〔侖〕
沦〔淪〕
轮〔輪〕
图〔圇〕
纶〔綸〕
伦〔倫〕

论〔論〕
luo
骡〔騾〕
脶〔腡〕
*罗〔羅〕
〔囉〕
逻〔邏〕
萝〔蘿〕
锣〔鑼〕
箩〔籮〕
椤〔欏〕
猡〔玀〕
荦〔犖〕
泺〔濼〕
骆〔駱〕
络〔絡〕
M
m
呒〔嘸〕
ma
妈〔媽〕
*马〔馬〕
蚂〔螞〕
玛〔瑪〕
码〔碼〕
犸〔獁〕

骂〔罵〕
吗〔嗎〕
唛〔嘜〕
mai
*买〔買〕
*麦〔麥〕
*卖〔賣〕
迈〔邁〕
荬〔蕒〕
man
颟〔顢〕
馒〔饅〕
鳗〔鰻〕
蛮〔蠻〕
瞒〔瞞〕
满〔滿〕
螨〔蟎〕
谩〔謾〕
缦〔縵〕
镘〔鏝〕
mang
铓〔鋩〕
mao
锚〔錨〕
铆〔鉚〕
贸〔貿〕

me

么〔麼〕

mei

霉〔黴〕

镅〔鎇〕

鹛〔鶥〕

镁〔鎂〕

men

*门〔門〕

扪〔捫〕

钔〔鍆〕

懑〔懣〕

闷〔悶〕

焖〔燜〕

们〔們〕

meng

蒙〔矇〕

〔濛〕

〔懞〕

锰〔錳〕

梦〔夢〕

mi

谜〔謎〕

祢〔禰〕

弥〔彌〕

〔瀰〕

猕〔獼〕

谧〔謐〕

觅〔覓〕

mian

绵〔綿〕

渑〔澠〕

缅〔緬〕

面〔麵〕

miao

鹋〔鶓〕

缈〔緲〕

缪〔繆〕

庙〔廟〕

mie

灭〔滅〕

蔑〔衊〕

min

缗〔緡〕

闵〔閔〕

悯〔憫〕

闽〔閩〕

*黾〔黽〕

鳘〔鰵〕

ming

鸣〔鳴〕

铭〔銘〕

miu

谬〔謬〕

缪〔繆〕

mo

谟〔謨〕

馍〔饃〕

蓦〔驀〕

mou

谋〔謀〕

缪〔繆〕

mu

亩〔畝〕

钼〔鉬〕

N

na

镎〔鎿〕

钠〔鈉〕

纳〔納〕

nan

*难〔難〕

nang

馕〔饢〕

nao

挠〔撓〕

蛲〔蟯〕

铙〔鐃〕

恼〔惱〕

脑〔腦〕

闹〔鬧〕

ne

讷〔訥〕

nei

馁〔餒〕

neng

泞〔濘〕

ni

鲵〔鯢〕

铌〔鈮〕

拟〔擬〕

腻〔膩〕

nian

鲇〔鮎〕

鲶〔鯰〕

辇〔輦〕

撵〔攆〕

niang

酿〔釀〕

niao

*鸟〔鳥〕

茑〔蔦〕

袅〔裊〕

nie

*聂〔聶〕

颞〔顳〕

嗫〔囁〕

蹑〔躡〕

镊〔鑷〕

啮〔嚙〕

镍〔鎳〕

ning

*宁〔寧〕

柠〔檸〕

咛〔嚀〕

狞〔獰〕

聍〔聹〕

拧〔擰〕

泞〔濘〕

niu

钮〔鈕〕

纽〔紐〕

nong

*农〔農〕

浓〔濃〕

侬〔儂〕

脓〔膿〕

哝〔噥〕

nu

驽〔駑〕

nü

钕〔釹〕

nüe

疟〔瘧〕

nuo

傩〔儺〕
诺〔諾〕
锘〔鍩〕

O

ou

*区〔區〕
讴〔謳〕
瓯〔甌〕
鸥〔鷗〕
殴〔毆〕
欧〔歐〕
呕〔嘔〕
沤〔漚〕
怄〔慪〕

P

pan

蹒〔蹣〕

盘〔盤〕

pang

鳑〔鰟〕
庞〔龐〕

pei

赔〔賠〕
锫〔錇〕
辔〔轡〕

pen

喷〔噴〕

peng

鹏〔鵬〕

pi

纰〔紕〕
罴〔羆〕
鲏〔鮍〕
铍〔鈹〕
辟〔闢〕
鹏〔鶅〕

pian

骈〔駢〕
谝〔諞〕
骗〔騙〕

piao

飘〔飄〕
缥〔縹〕

骠〔驃〕

pin

嫔〔嬪〕
频〔頻〕
颦〔顰〕
贫〔貧〕

ping

评〔評〕
苹〔蘋〕
鲆〔鮃〕
凭〔憑〕

po

钋〔釙〕
颇〔頗〕
泼〔潑〕
钹〔鏺〕
钷〔鉕〕

pu

铺〔鋪〕
扑〔撲〕
仆〔僕〕
镤〔鏷〕
谱〔譜〕
镨〔錯〕
朴〔樸〕

Q

qi

缉〔緝〕
桤〔榿〕
*齐〔齊〕
蛴〔蠐〕
脐〔臍〕
骑〔騎〕
骐〔騏〕
鳍〔鰭〕
颀〔頎〕
蕲〔蘄〕
启〔啓〕
绮〔綺〕
*岂〔豈〕
碛〔磧〕
*气〔氣〕
讫〔訖〕
荠〔薺〕

qian

骞〔騫〕
谦〔謙〕
悭〔慳〕
牵〔牽〕
*佥〔僉〕

签〔簽〕
〔籤〕

qi

千〔韆〕
*迁〔遷〕
钎〔釺〕
铅〔鉛〕
鸽〔鵮〕
荨〔蕁〕
钳〔鉗〕
钱〔錢〕
钤〔鈐〕
浅〔淺〕
谴〔譴〕
缱〔繾〕
堑〔塹〕
椠〔槧〕
纤〔縴〕

qiang

玱〔瑲〕
枪〔槍〕
锵〔鏘〕
墙〔牆〕
蔷〔薔〕
樯〔檣〕
嫱〔嬙〕
镪〔鏹〕

13

羟〔羥〕
抢〔搶〕
炝〔熗〕
戗〔戧〕
跄〔蹌〕
呛〔嗆〕

qiao

硗〔磽〕
跷〔蹺〕
锹〔鍬〕
缲〔繰〕
翘〔翹〕
*乔〔喬〕
桥〔橋〕
硚〔礄〕
侨〔僑〕
鞒〔鞽〕
荞〔蕎〕
谯〔譙〕
*壳〔殼〕
窍〔竅〕
诮〔誚〕

qie

锲〔鍥〕
惬〔愜〕
箧〔篋〕

窃〔竊〕

qin

*亲〔親〕
钦〔欽〕
嵚〔嶔〕
骎〔駸〕
寝〔寢〕
锓〔鋟〕
揿〔撳〕

qing

鲭〔鯖〕
轻〔輕〕
氢〔氫〕
倾〔傾〕
赪〔賾〕
请〔請〕
顷〔頃〕
庼〔廎〕
庆〔慶〕

qiong

*穷〔窮〕
䓖〔藭〕
琼〔瓊〕
茕〔煢〕

qiu

秋〔鞦〕

鹙〔鶖〕
鳅〔鰍〕
鳍〔鰭〕
巯〔巰〕

qu

曲〔麯〕
*区〔區〕
驱〔驅〕
岖〔嶇〕
躯〔軀〕
诎〔詘〕
趋〔趨〕
鸲〔鴝〕
龋〔齲〕
觑〔覷〕
阒〔闃〕

quan

权〔權〕
颧〔顴〕
铨〔銓〕
诠〔詮〕
绻〔綣〕
劝〔勸〕

que

悫〔慤〕
鹊〔鵲〕

阙〔闕〕
确〔確〕
阕〔闋〕

R

rang

让〔讓〕

rao

桡〔橈〕
荛〔蕘〕
饶〔饒〕
娆〔嬈〕
扰〔擾〕
绕〔繞〕

re

热〔熱〕

ren

认〔認〕
饪〔飪〕
纴〔紝〕
轫〔軔〕
纫〔紉〕
韧〔韌〕

rong

荣〔榮〕
蝾〔蠑〕

嵘〔嶸〕
绒〔絨〕

ru

铷〔銣〕
颥〔顬〕
缛〔縟〕

ruan

软〔軟〕

rui

锐〔銳〕

run

闰〔閏〕
润〔潤〕

S

sa

洒〔灑〕
飒〔颯〕
萨〔薩〕

sai

鳃〔鰓〕
赛〔賽〕

san

毵〔毿〕
馓〔饊〕
伞〔傘〕

sang

丧〔喪〕
颡〔顙〕

sao

骚〔騷〕
缫〔繅〕
扫〔掃〕

se

涩〔澀〕
*啬〔嗇〕
穑〔穡〕
铯〔銫〕

sha

鲨〔鯊〕
纱〔紗〕
*杀〔殺〕
铩〔鎩〕

shai

筛〔篩〕
晒〔曬〕

shan

钐〔釤〕
陕〔陝〕
闪〔閃〕
镨〔鐥〕
鳝〔鱔〕

缮〔繕〕
掸〔撣〕
骟〔騸〕
镐〔鎬〕
禅〔禪〕
讪〔訕〕
赡〔贍〕

shang

殇〔殤〕
觞〔觴〕
伤〔傷〕
赏〔賞〕

shao

烧〔燒〕
绍〔紹〕

she

赊〔賒〕
舍〔捨〕
设〔設〕
滠〔灄〕
慑〔懾〕
摄〔攝〕
库〔厙〕

shei

谁〔誰〕

shen

绅〔紳〕
*参〔參〕
糁〔糝〕
*审〔審〕
谉〔讅〕
婶〔嬸〕
沈〔瀋〕
谂〔諗〕
肾〔腎〕
渗〔滲〕
瘆〔瘮〕

sheng

声〔聲〕
渑〔澠〕
绳〔繩〕
胜〔勝〕
*圣〔聖〕

shi

湿〔濕〕
诗〔詩〕
*师〔師〕
浉〔溮〕
狮〔獅〕
鸤〔鳲〕
实〔實〕

埘〔塒〕
鲥〔鰣〕
识〔識〕
*时〔時〕
蚀〔蝕〕
驶〔駛〕
铈〔鈰〕
视〔視〕
谥〔謚〕
试〔試〕
轼〔軾〕
势〔勢〕
莳〔蒔〕
贳〔貰〕
释〔釋〕
饰〔飾〕
适〔適〕

shou

兽〔獸〕
*寿〔壽〕
绶〔綬〕

shu

枢〔樞〕
摅〔攄〕
输〔輸〕
纾〔紓〕

书〔書〕
赎〔贖〕
*属〔屬〕
数〔數〕
树〔樹〕
术〔術〕
竖〔豎〕

shuai

帅〔帥〕

shuan

闩〔閂〕

shuang

*双〔雙〕
泷〔瀧〕

shui

谁〔誰〕

shun

顺〔順〕

shuo

说〔說〕
硕〔碩〕
烁〔爍〕
铄〔鑠〕

si

锶〔鍶〕
飔〔颸〕

酾〔釃〕　诉〔訴〕　挞〔撻〕　傥〔儻〕　**tiao**
缌〔緦〕　*肃〔肅〕　阘〔闒〕　镗〔钂〕　*条〔條〕
丝〔絲〕　**sui**　**tai**　烫〔燙〕　鲦〔鰷〕
咝〔噝〕　虽〔雖〕　台〔臺〕　**tao**　龆〔齠〕
鸶〔鷥〕　随〔隨〕　〔檯〕　涛〔濤〕　调〔調〕
蛳〔螄〕　绥〔綏〕　〔颱〕　韬〔韜〕　棠〔糶〕
驷〔駟〕　*岁〔歲〕　骀〔駘〕　绦〔縧〕　**tie**
饲〔飼〕　详〔諙〕　鲐〔鮐〕　焘〔燾〕　贴〔貼〕
song　**sun**　态〔態〕　讨〔討〕　铁〔鐵〕
松〔鬆〕　*孙〔孫〕　钛〔鈦〕　**te**　**ting**
怂〔慫〕　荪〔蓀〕　**tan**　铽〔鋱〕　厅〔廳〕
耸〔聳〕　狲〔猻〕　滩〔灘〕　**teng**　烃〔烴〕
扨〔摋〕　损〔損〕　瘫〔癱〕　誊〔謄〕　听〔聽〕
讼〔訟〕　**suo**　摊〔攤〕　腾〔騰〕　颋〔頲〕
颂〔頌〕　缩〔縮〕　贪〔貪〕　螣〔縢〕　铤〔鋌〕
诵〔誦〕　琐〔瑣〕　谈〔談〕　**ti**　**tong**
sou　唢〔嗩〕　坛〔壇〕　锑〔銻〕　铜〔銅〕
馊〔餿〕　锁〔鎖〕　〔罎〕　鹈〔鶗〕　鲖〔鮦〕
锼〔鎪〕　苏〔嚕〕　谭〔譚〕　鹈〔鵜〕　统〔統〕
飕〔颼〕　　　昙〔曇〕　绨〔綈〕　恸〔慟〕
薮〔藪〕　**T**　弹〔彈〕　缇〔緹〕　**tou**
擞〔擻〕　　　钽〔鉭〕　题〔題〕　头〔頭〕
su　**ta**　叹〔嘆〕　体〔體〕　**tu**
苏〔蘇〕　铊〔鉈〕　**tang**　**tian**　图〔圖〕
稣〔穌〕　鳎〔鰨〕　镗〔鏜〕　阗〔闐〕　涂〔塗〕
谡〔謖〕　獭〔獺〕　汤〔湯〕　　　钍〔釷〕
　　达〔澾〕

16

tuan
抟〔摶〕
团〔團〕
〔糰〕
tui
颓〔頹〕
tun
饨〔飩〕
tuo
饦〔飥〕
驼〔駝〕
鸵〔鴕〕
驮〔馱〕
鼍〔鼉〕
椭〔橢〕
萚〔蘀〕
箨〔籜〕
W
wa
娲〔媧〕
洼〔窪〕
袜〔襪〕
wai
呙〔喎〕
wan
弯〔彎〕

湾〔灣〕
纨〔紈〕
顽〔頑〕
绾〔綰〕
*万〔萬〕
wang
网〔網〕
辋〔輞〕
wei
*为〔爲〕
维〔維〕
潍〔濰〕
*韦〔韋〕
违〔違〕
围〔圍〕
涠〔潿〕
帏〔幃〕
闱〔闈〕
伪〔偽〕
鲔〔鮪〕
诿〔諉〕
炜〔煒〕
玮〔瑋〕
苇〔葦〕
韪〔韙〕
伟〔偉〕

纬〔緯〕
硙〔磑〕
谓〔謂〕
卫〔衛〕
wen
鳁〔鰛〕
纹〔紋〕
闻〔聞〕
阌〔閿〕
稳〔穩〕
问〔問〕
wo
涡〔渦〕
窝〔窩〕
莴〔萵〕
蜗〔蝸〕
挝〔撾〕
龌〔齷〕
wu
诬〔誣〕
*乌〔烏〕
呜〔嗚〕
钨〔鎢〕
邬〔鄔〕
*无〔無〕
芜〔蕪〕

妩〔嫵〕
怃〔憮〕
庑〔廡〕
鹉〔鵡〕
坞〔塢〕
务〔務〕
雾〔霧〕
鹜〔鶩〕
骛〔騖〕
误〔誤〕
X
xi
牺〔犧〕
饻〔餏〕
锡〔錫〕
袭〔襲〕
觋〔覡〕
习〔習〕
鳛〔鰼〕
玺〔璽〕
铣〔銑〕
系〔係〕
〔繫〕
细〔細〕
阋〔鬩〕

妩〔嫵〕
忾〔愾〕
庑〔廡〕
鹉〔鵡〕
坞〔塢〕
务〔務〕
雾〔霧〕
鹜〔鶩〕
骛〔騖〕
误〔誤〕

妩〔嫵〕
妩〔嫵〕
妩〔嫵〕
妩〔嫵〕
妩〔嫵〕
妩〔嫵〕
妩〔嫵〕
妩〔嫵〕

娬
娬
娬
娬

	xiao	谢〔謝〕	项〔項〕	讯〔訊〕
显〔顯〕	骁〔驍〕	xin	续〔續〕	逊〔遜〕
险〔險〕	哓〔嘵〕	锌〔鋅〕	绪〔緒〕	
狝〔獮〕	销〔銷〕	䜣〔訢〕	xuan	**Y**
铣〔銑〕	绡〔綃〕	衅〔釁〕	轩〔軒〕	
*献〔獻〕	嚣〔囂〕	xing	谖〔諼〕	**ya**
线〔綫〕	枭〔梟〕	兴〔興〕	悬〔懸〕	压〔壓〕
现〔現〕	鸮〔鴞〕	荥〔滎〕	选〔選〕	鸦〔鴉〕
苋〔莧〕	萧〔蕭〕	钘〔鈃〕	癣〔癬〕	鸭〔鴨〕
岘〔峴〕	潇〔瀟〕	铏〔鉶〕	旋〔鏇〕	钘〔釾〕
县〔縣〕	蟏〔蠨〕	陉〔陘〕	铉〔鉉〕	哑〔啞〕
宪〔憲〕	箫〔簫〕	饧〔餳〕	绚〔絢〕	氩〔氬〕
馅〔餡〕	晓〔曉〕	xiong	xue	*亚〔亞〕
xiang	啸〔嘯〕	讻〔訩〕	学〔學〕	垭〔埡〕
骧〔驤〕	xie	诇〔詗〕	峃〔嶨〕	挜〔掗〕
镶〔鑲〕	颉〔頡〕	xiu	鳕〔鱈〕	娅〔婭〕
*乡〔鄉〕	撷〔擷〕	馐〔饈〕	谑〔謔〕	讶〔訝〕
芗〔薌〕	缬〔纈〕	鸺〔鵂〕	xun	轧〔軋〕
缃〔緗〕	协〔協〕	绣〔綉〕	勋〔勛〕	yan
详〔詳〕	挟〔挾〕	锈〔銹〕	埙〔塤〕	
鲞〔鯗〕	胁〔脅〕	xu	驯〔馴〕	阀〔閼〕
响〔響〕	谐〔諧〕	须〔須〕	询〔詢〕	阉〔閹〕
饷〔餉〕	*写〔寫〕	〔鬚〕	*寻〔尋〕	恹〔懨〕
飨〔饗〕	亵〔褻〕	谞〔諝〕	浔〔潯〕	颜〔顏〕
向〔嚮〕	泻〔瀉〕	许〔許〕	鲟〔鱘〕	盐〔鹽〕
象〔像〕	绁〔紲〕	诩〔詡〕	训〔訓〕	*严〔嚴〕
项〔項〕				阎〔閻〕

18

厣〔厴〕 痒〔癢〕 医〔醫〕 亿〔億〕 荧〔熒〕
黡〔黶〕 养〔養〕 鹥〔鷖〕 忆〔憶〕 莹〔瑩〕
魇〔魘〕 样〔樣〕 袆〔褘〕 诣〔詣〕 茔〔塋〕

yao

俨〔儼〕 *尧〔堯〕 颐〔頤〕 镱〔鐿〕 萤〔螢〕
龚〔龔〕 峣〔嶢〕 遗〔遺〕 萦〔縈〕

yin

谚〔諺〕 谣〔謠〕 仪〔儀〕 铟〔銦〕 营〔營〕
谳〔讞〕 铫〔銚〕 诒〔詒〕 *阴〔陰〕 赢〔贏〕
*厌〔厭〕 轺〔軺〕 贻〔貽〕 荫〔蔭〕 蝇〔蠅〕
餍〔饜〕 疟〔瘧〕 饴〔飴〕 龈〔齦〕 瘿〔癭〕
赝〔贋〕 鹞〔鷂〕 蚁〔蟻〕 银〔銀〕 颖〔穎〕
艳〔艷〕 钥〔鑰〕 钇〔釔〕 饮〔飲〕 颍〔潁〕
滟〔灩〕 药〔藥〕 谊〔誼〕 *隐〔隱〕

yo

谳〔讞〕 瘗〔瘞〕 瘾〔癮〕 哟〔喲〕

ye

镒〔鎰〕 卿〔朐〕

yong

砚〔硯〕 爷〔爺〕 缢〔縊〕 痈〔癰〕
觃〔覎〕 靥〔靨〕 勚〔勩〕

ying

拥〔擁〕
酽〔釅〕 *页〔頁〕 怿〔懌〕 应〔應〕 佣〔傭〕
验〔驗〕 烨〔燁〕 译〔譯〕 鹰〔鷹〕 镛〔鏞〕

yang

晔〔曄〕 驿〔驛〕 莺〔鶯〕 鳙〔鱅〕
鸯〔鴦〕 *业〔業〕 峄〔嶧〕 罂〔罌〕 颙〔顒〕
疡〔瘍〕 邺〔鄴〕 绎〔繹〕 婴〔嬰〕 踊〔踴〕
炀〔煬〕 叶〔葉〕 *义〔義〕 璎〔瓔〕

you

杨〔楊〕 谒〔謁〕 议〔議〕 樱〔櫻〕 忧〔憂〕
扬〔揚〕 轶〔軼〕 撄〔攖〕 优〔優〕

yi

旸〔暘〕 *艺〔藝〕 嘤〔嚶〕 鱿〔魷〕
钖〔錫〕 铱〔銥〕 呓〔囈〕 鹦〔鸚〕 *犹〔猶〕
阳〔陽〕 缨〔纓〕

异〔異〕

19

莸〔蕕〕	妪〔嫗〕	阅〔閱〕	**zai**	泽〔澤〕
铀〔鈾〕	郁〔鬱〕	钺〔鉞〕	载〔載〕	择〔擇〕
邮〔郵〕	谕〔諭〕	跃〔躍〕	**zan**	**zei**
铕〔銪〕	鹆〔鵒〕	*乐〔樂〕	趱〔趲〕	贼〔賊〕
诱〔誘〕	饫〔飫〕	钥〔鑰〕	攒〔攢〕	**zen**
yu	狱〔獄〕	**yun**	錾〔鏨〕	谮〔譖〕
纡〔紆〕	预〔預〕	*云〔雲〕	暂〔暫〕	**zeng**
舆〔輿〕	滪〔澦〕	芸〔蕓〕	赞〔贊〕	缯〔繒〕
欤〔歟〕	蓣〔蕷〕	纭〔紜〕	瓒〔瓚〕	赠〔贈〕
余〔餘〕	鹬〔鷸〕	陨〔隕〕	**zang**	锃〔鋥〕
觎〔覦〕	**yuan**	郧〔鄖〕	赃〔臟〕	**zha**
谀〔諛〕	渊〔淵〕	殒〔殞〕	脏〔臟〕	铡〔鍘〕
*鱼〔魚〕	鸢〔鳶〕	陨〔隕〕	〔髒〕	闸〔閘〕
渔〔漁〕	鸳〔鴛〕	恽〔惲〕	驵〔駔〕	轧〔軋〕
歔〔歔〕	鼋〔黿〕	晕〔暈〕	**zao**	鲝〔鮺〕
*与〔與〕	园〔園〕	郓〔鄆〕	凿〔鑿〕	鲊〔鮓〕
语〔語〕	辕〔轅〕	运〔運〕	枣〔棗〕	诈〔詐〕
龉〔齬〕	员〔員〕	酝〔醞〕	灶〔竈〕	**zhai**
伛〔傴〕	圆〔圓〕	韫〔韞〕	**ze**	斋〔齋〕
屿〔嶼〕	缘〔緣〕	缊〔縕〕	责〔責〕	债〔債〕
誉〔譽〕	橼〔櫞〕	蕴〔蘊〕	赜〔賾〕	**zhan**
钰〔鈺〕	远〔遠〕		啧〔嘖〕	鹯〔鸇〕
吁〔籲〕	愿〔願〕	**Z**	帻〔幘〕	鳣〔鱣〕
御〔禦〕	**yue**		箦〔簀〕	毡〔氈〕
驭〔馭〕	约〔約〕	**za**	则〔則〕	觇〔覘〕
阈〔閾〕	哕〔噦〕	臜〔臢〕	鲗〔鯽〕	谵〔譫〕

20

斩〔斬〕
崭〔嶄〕
盏〔盞〕
辗〔輾〕
绽〔綻〕
颤〔顫〕
栈〔棧〕
战〔戰〕

zhang

张〔張〕
*长〔長〕
涨〔漲〕
帐〔帳〕
账〔賬〕
胀〔脹〕

zhao

钊〔釗〕
赵〔趙〕
诏〔詔〕

zhe

谪〔謫〕
辙〔轍〕
蛰〔蟄〕
辄〔輒〕
詟〔讋〕
折〔摺〕

锗〔鍺〕
这〔這〕
鹧〔鷓〕

zhen

针〔針〕
贞〔貞〕
浈〔湞〕
祯〔禎〕
桢〔楨〕
侦〔偵〕
缜〔縝〕
诊〔診〕
轸〔軫〕
鸩〔鴆〕
赈〔賑〕
镇〔鎮〕
纼〔紖〕
阵〔陣〕

zheng

钲〔鉦〕
征〔徵〕
铮〔錚〕
症〔癥〕
*郑〔鄭〕
证〔證〕

帧〔幀〕
诤〔諍〕
阐〔闡〕

zhi

只〔隻〕
〔衹〕
织〔織〕
职〔職〕
踯〔躑〕
*执〔執〕
絷〔縶〕
纸〔紙〕
挚〔摯〕
贽〔贄〕
鸷〔鷙〕
掷〔擲〕
滞〔滯〕
栉〔櫛〕
轾〔輊〕
致〔緻〕
帜〔幟〕
制〔製〕
*质〔質〕
踬〔躓〕
锧〔鑕〕
鸷〔騺〕

zhong

终〔終〕
钟〔鐘〕
〔鍾〕
种〔種〕
肿〔腫〕
众〔衆〕

zhou

诌〔謅〕
赒〔賙〕
鸼〔鵃〕
轴〔軸〕
纣〔紂〕
荮〔葤〕
骤〔驟〕
皱〔皺〕
绉〔縐〕
㤘〔㥮〕
㑇〔㑇〕
昼〔晝〕

zhu

诸〔諸〕
槠〔櫧〕
朱〔硃〕
诛〔誅〕
铢〔銖〕

烛〔燭〕
嘱〔囑〕
瞩〔矚〕
贮〔貯〕
驻〔駐〕
铸〔鑄〕
筑〔築〕

zhua

挝〔撾〕

zhuan

*专〔專〕
砖〔磚〕
䏝〔膞〕
颛〔顓〕
转〔轉〕
啭〔囀〕
赚〔賺〕
传〔傳〕
馔〔饌〕

zhuang

妆〔妝〕
装〔裝〕
庄〔莊〕
桩〔樁〕
戆〔戇〕
壮〔壯〕

21

状〔狀〕

zhui

骓〔騅〕

锥〔錐〕

赘〔贅〕

缒〔縋〕

缀〔綴〕

坠〔墜〕

zhun

谆〔諄〕

准〔準〕

zhuo

锗〔鐯〕

浊〔濁〕

诼〔諑〕

镯〔鐲〕

zi

谘〔諮〕

资〔資〕

镃〔鎡〕

觜〔觜〕

韬〔韜〕

锱〔錙〕

缁〔緇〕

鲻〔鯔〕

渍〔漬〕

zong

综〔綜〕

枞〔樅〕

总〔總〕

纵〔縱〕

zou

诹〔諏〕

鲰〔鯫〕

驺〔騶〕

邹〔鄒〕

zu

镞〔鏃〕

诅〔詛〕

组〔組〕

zuan

钻〔鑽〕

躜〔躦〕

缵〔纘〕

赚〔賺〕

zun

鳟〔鱒〕

zuo

凿〔鑿〕

B. 从简体查繁体

2 笔

厂〔廠〕
卜〔蔔〕
儿〔兒〕
*几〔幾〕
了〔瞭〕

3 笔

干〔乾〕
　〔幹〕
亏〔虧〕
才〔纔〕
*万〔萬〕
*与〔與〕
千〔韆〕
亿〔億〕

个〔個〕
么〔麼〕
*广〔廣〕
*门〔門〕
*义〔義〕
卫〔衛〕
飞〔飛〕
习〔習〕
*马〔馬〕
*乡〔鄉〕

4 笔

【一】

*丰〔豐〕
开〔開〕
*无〔無〕
*韦〔韋〕

*专〔專〕
*云〔雲〕
*艺〔藝〕
厅〔廳〕
*历〔歷〕
　〔曆〕
*区〔區〕
*车〔車〕

【丨】

*冈〔岡〕
*贝〔貝〕
*见〔見〕

【丿】

*气〔氣〕
*长〔長〕
仆〔僕〕
币〔幣〕

*从〔從〕
*仑〔侖〕
*仓〔倉〕
*风〔風〕
仅〔僅〕
凤〔鳳〕
*乌〔烏〕

【丶】

闩〔閂〕
*为〔爲〕
斗〔鬥〕
忆〔憶〕
订〔訂〕
计〔計〕
讣〔訃〕
认〔認〕
讥〔譏〕

【乛】

丑〔醜〕
*队〔隊〕
办〔辦〕
邓〔鄧〕
劝〔勸〕
*双〔雙〕
书〔書〕

5 笔

【一】

击〔擊〕
*戋〔戔〕
扑〔撲〕
*节〔節〕
术〔術〕
*龙〔龍〕

厉〔厲〕　务〔務〕　【乛】　扫〔掃〕　*当〔當〕
灭〔滅〕　*刍〔芻〕　辽〔遼〕　扬〔揚〕　〔噹〕
*东〔東〕　饥〔饑〕　*边〔邊〕　场〔場〕　尘〔塵〕
轧〔軋〕　　　出〔齣〕　*亚〔亞〕　吁〔籲〕
【丨】　【丶】　*发〔發〕　芗〔薌〕　吓〔嚇〕
*卢〔盧〕　邝〔鄺〕　〔髮〕　朴〔樸〕　*虫〔蟲〕
*业〔業〕　冯〔馮〕　*圣〔聖〕　机〔機〕　曲〔麯〕
旧〔舊〕　闪〔閃〕　*对〔對〕　权〔權〕　团〔團〕
帅〔帥〕　兰〔蘭〕　台〔臺〕　*过〔過〕　〔糰〕
*归〔歸〕　*汇〔匯〕　〔檯〕　协〔協〕　吗〔嗎〕
叶〔葉〕　〔彙〕　〔颱〕　压〔壓〕　屿〔嶼〕
号〔號〕　头〔頭〕　纠〔糾〕　*厌〔厭〕　*岁〔歲〕
电〔電〕　汉〔漢〕　驭〔馭〕　厍〔厙〕　回〔迴〕
只〔隻〕　*宁〔寧〕　丝〔絲〕　*页〔頁〕　*岂〔豈〕
〔衹〕　评〔許〕　　夸〔誇〕　则〔則〕
叽〔嘰〕　讧〔訌〕　**6 笔**　夺〔奪〕　刚〔剛〕
叹〔嘆〕　讨〔討〕　【一】　*达〔達〕　网〔網〕
【丿】　*写〔寫〕　　*夹〔夾〕　【丿】
们〔們〕　让〔讓〕　玑〔璣〕　轨〔軌〕　钆〔釓〕
仪〔儀〕　礼〔禮〕　*动〔動〕　*尧〔堯〕　钇〔釔〕
丛〔叢〕　讪〔訕〕　*执〔執〕　划〔劃〕　朱〔硃〕
*尔〔爾〕　讫〔訖〕　巩〔鞏〕　迈〔邁〕　*迁〔遷〕
*乐〔樂〕　训〔訓〕　圹〔壙〕　*毕〔畢〕　*乔〔喬〕
处〔處〕　议〔議〕　扩〔擴〕　【丨】　伟〔偉〕
冬〔鼕〕　讯〔訊〕　扪〔捫〕　贞〔貞〕　传〔傳〕
*鸟〔鳥〕　记〔記〕　　*师〔師〕　伛〔傴〕

优〔優〕	【丶】	讹〔訛〕	纡〔紆〕	运〔運〕
伤〔傷〕		诉〔訴〕	红〔紅〕	抚〔撫〕
伥〔倀〕	壮〔壯〕	论〔論〕	纣〔紂〕	坛〔壇〕
价〔價〕	冲〔衝〕	讻〔詾〕	驮〔馱〕	〔罎〕
伦〔倫〕	妆〔妝〕	讼〔訟〕	纤〔縴〕	抟〔摶〕
伧〔傖〕	庄〔莊〕	讽〔諷〕	〔纖〕	坏〔壞〕
*华〔華〕	庆〔慶〕	*农〔農〕	纥〔紇〕	抠〔摳〕
伙〔夥〕	*刘〔劉〕	设〔設〕	驯〔馴〕	坜〔壢〕
伪〔偽〕	*齐〔齊〕	访〔訪〕	纨〔紈〕	扰〔擾〕
向〔嚮〕	*产〔產〕	诀〔訣〕	约〔約〕	坝〔壩〕
后〔後〕	闭〔閉〕	【一】	级〔級〕	贡〔貢〕
*会〔會〕	问〔問〕	*寻〔尋〕	纩〔纊〕	㧑〔撝〕
*杀〔殺〕	闯〔闖〕	*尽〔盡〕	纪〔紀〕	折〔摺〕
合〔閤〕	关〔關〕	〔儘〕	驰〔馳〕	抡〔掄〕
众〔衆〕	灯〔燈〕	导〔導〕	纫〔紉〕	抢〔搶〕
爷〔爺〕	汤〔湯〕	*孙〔孫〕		坞〔塢〕
伞〔傘〕	忏〔懺〕	阵〔陣〕	**7 笔**	坟〔墳〕
创〔創〕	兴〔興〕	阳〔陽〕		护〔護〕
杂〔雜〕	讲〔講〕	阶〔階〕	【一】	*壳〔殻〕
负〔負〕	讳〔諱〕	*阴〔陰〕	*寿〔壽〕	块〔塊〕
犷〔獷〕	讴〔謳〕	妇〔婦〕	*麦〔麥〕	声〔聲〕
犸〔獁〕	军〔軍〕	妈〔媽〕	玛〔瑪〕	报〔報〕
凫〔鳧〕	讵〔詎〕	戏〔戲〕	*进〔進〕	拟〔擬〕
邬〔鄔〕	讶〔訝〕	观〔觀〕	远〔遠〕	㧑〔攛〕
饦〔飥〕	讷〔訥〕	欢〔歡〕	违〔違〕	芜〔蕪〕
饧〔餳〕	许〔許〕	*买〔買〕	韧〔韌〕	苇〔葦〕
			划〔劃〕	

25

芸〔蕓〕　【丨】　财〔財〕　*犹〔猶〕　闰〔閏〕
苈〔藶〕　*卤〔鹵〕　囵〔圇〕　狈〔狽〕　闱〔闈〕
苋〔莧〕　〔滷〕　觃〔覎〕　鸠〔鳩〕　闲〔閑〕
苁〔蓯〕　邺〔鄴〕　帏〔幃〕　*条〔條〕　间〔間〕
苍〔蒼〕　坚〔堅〕　岖〔嶇〕　岛〔島〕　闵〔閔〕
*严〔嚴〕　*时〔時〕　岗〔崗〕　邹〔鄒〕　闷〔悶〕
芦〔蘆〕　呒〔嘸〕　岘〔峴〕　饨〔飩〕　灿〔燦〕
劳〔勞〕　县〔縣〕　帐〔帳〕　饩〔餼〕　灶〔竈〕
克〔剋〕　里〔裏〕　岚〔嵐〕　饪〔飪〕　炀〔煬〕
苏〔蘇〕　呓〔囈〕　【丿】　饫〔飫〕　沣〔灃〕
〔囌〕　呕〔嘔〕　针〔針〕　饬〔飭〕　沤〔漚〕
极〔極〕　园〔園〕　钉〔釘〕　饭〔飯〕　沥〔瀝〕
杨〔楊〕　呖〔嚦〕　钊〔釗〕　饮〔飲〕　沦〔淪〕
*两〔兩〕　旷〔曠〕　钋〔釙〕　系〔係〕　沧〔滄〕
*丽〔麗〕　围〔圍〕　钌〔釬〕　〔繫〕　沨〔渢〕
医〔醫〕　吨〔噸〕　乱〔亂〕　【丶】　沟〔溝〕
励〔勵〕　旸〔暘〕　体〔體〕　冻〔凍〕　沩〔溈〕
还〔還〕　邮〔郵〕　佣〔傭〕　状〔狀〕　沪〔滬〕
矶〔磯〕　困〔睏〕　伤〔傷〕　亩〔畝〕　沈〔瀋〕
奁〔奩〕　员〔員〕　彻〔徹〕　庑〔廡〕　怃〔憮〕
歼〔殲〕　呗〔唄〕　余〔餘〕　库〔庫〕　怀〔懷〕
*来〔來〕　听〔聽〕　*佥〔僉〕　疖〔癤〕　怄〔慪〕
欤〔歟〕　呛〔嗆〕　谷〔穀〕　疗〔療〕　忧〔憂〕
轩〔軒〕　呜〔嗚〕　邻〔鄰〕　应〔應〕　忾〔愾〕
连〔連〕　别〔彆〕　肠〔腸〕　这〔這〕　怅〔悵〕
轫〔軔〕　　*龟〔龜〕　庐〔廬〕　怆〔愴〕

26

*穷〔窮〕
证〔證〕
诂〔詁〕
诃〔訶〕
启〔啓〕
评〔評〕
补〔補〕
诅〔詛〕
识〔識〕
诇〔詗〕
诈〔詐〕
诉〔訴〕
诊〔診〕
诋〔詆〕
诌〔謅〕
词〔詞〕
诎〔詘〕
诏〔詔〕
译〔譯〕
诒〔詒〕

【乛】
*灵〔靈〕
层〔層〕
迟〔遲〕
张〔張〕
际〔際〕

陆〔陸〕
陇〔隴〕
陈〔陳〕
坠〔墜〕
陉〔陘〕
妪〔嫗〕
妩〔嫵〕
妫〔嬀〕
刭〔剄〕
劲〔勁〕
鸡〔鷄〕
纬〔緯〕
绉〔縐〕
驱〔驅〕
纯〔純〕
纰〔紕〕
纱〔紗〕
纲〔綱〕
纳〔納〕
纴〔紝〕
驳〔駁〕
纵〔縱〕
纶〔綸〕
纷〔紛〕
纸〔紙〕
纹〔紋〕

纺〔紡〕
驴〔驢〕
纠〔糾〕
纽〔紐〕
纾〔紓〕

8 笔

【一】
玮〔瑋〕
环〔環〕
责〔責〕
现〔現〕
表〔錶〕
珑〔瓏〕
规〔規〕
匦〔匭〕
拢〔攏〕
拣〔揀〕
垆〔壚〕
担〔擔〕
顶〔頂〕
拥〔擁〕
势〔勢〕
拦〔攔〕
㧑〔撝〕
拧〔擰〕

拨〔撥〕
择〔擇〕
茏〔蘢〕
苹〔蘋〕
茑〔蔦〕
范〔範〕
茔〔塋〕
茕〔煢〕
茎〔莖〕
枢〔樞〕
枥〔櫪〕
柜〔櫃〕
枨〔棖〕
板〔闆〕
枞〔樅〕
松〔鬆〕
枪〔槍〕
枫〔楓〕
构〔構〕
丧〔喪〕
*画〔畫〕
枣〔棗〕
*卖〔賣〕
郁〔鬱〕

矾〔礬〕
矿〔礦〕
砀〔碭〕
码〔碼〕
厕〔廁〕
奋〔奮〕
态〔態〕
瓯〔甌〕
欧〔歐〕
殴〔毆〕
垄〔壟〕
郏〔郟〕
轰〔轟〕
顷〔頃〕
转〔轉〕
轭〔軛〕
斩〔斬〕
轮〔輪〕
软〔軟〕
鸢〔鳶〕

【丨】
*齿〔齒〕
*虏〔虜〕
肾〔腎〕
贤〔賢〕
昙〔曇〕

27

*国〔國〕　【丿】　径〔徑〕　饴〔飴〕　泾〔涇〕
畅〔暢〕　钍〔釷〕　舍〔捨〕　【丶】　怜〔憐〕
咙〔嚨〕　钎〔釺〕　剑〔劍〕　变〔變〕　㤘〔㥄〕
虮〔蟣〕　钏〔釧〕　郐〔鄶〕　庞〔龐〕　怿〔懌〕
*鼋〔黿〕　钗〔釵〕　怂〔慫〕　庙〔廟〕　峃〔嶨〕
鸣〔鳴〕　钓〔釣〕　籴〔糴〕　疟〔瘧〕　学〔學〕
咛〔嚀〕　钒〔釩〕　觅〔覓〕　疠〔癘〕　宝〔寶〕
咝〔噝〕　钔〔鍆〕　贪〔貪〕　疡〔瘍〕　宠〔寵〕
*罗〔羅〕　钕〔釹〕　贫〔貧〕　剂〔劑〕　*审〔審〕
〔囉〕　钖〔錫〕　饯〔餞〕　废〔廢〕　帘〔簾〕
崃〔崍〕　钗〔釵〕　肤〔膚〕　闸〔閘〕　实〔實〕
岿〔巋〕　制〔製〕　胪〔臚〕　闹〔鬧〕　诓〔誆〕
帜〔幟〕　迭〔疊〕　肿〔腫〕　*郑〔鄭〕　诔〔誄〕
岭〔嶺〕　刮〔颳〕　胀〔脹〕　卷〔捲〕　试〔試〕
刿〔劌〕　侠〔俠〕　肮〔骯〕　炜〔煒〕　诖〔詿〕
剀〔剴〕　侥〔僥〕　胁〔脅〕　炝〔熗〕　诗〔詩〕
凯〔凱〕　侦〔偵〕　迩〔邇〕　炉〔爐〕　诘〔詰〕
峄〔嶧〕　侧〔側〕　*鱼〔魚〕　浅〔淺〕　诙〔詼〕
败〔敗〕　凭〔憑〕　狞〔獰〕　泷〔瀧〕　诚〔誠〕
账〔賬〕　侨〔僑〕　*备〔備〕　泸〔瀘〕　郓〔鄆〕
贩〔販〕　侩〔儈〕　枭〔梟〕　泺〔濼〕　衬〔襯〕
贬〔貶〕　货〔貨〕　饯〔餞〕　泞〔濘〕　祎〔禕〕
贮〔貯〕　侪〔儕〕　饰〔飾〕　泻〔瀉〕　视〔視〕
图〔圖〕　侬〔儂〕　饱〔飽〕　泼〔潑〕　诛〔誅〕
购〔購〕　*质〔質〕　饲〔飼〕　泽〔澤〕　话〔話〕
　　　　征〔徵〕　饳〔飿〕　　　　诞〔誕〕

28

诟〔詬〕 绂〔紱〕 贯〔貫〕 荚〔莢〕 栈〔棧〕
诠〔詮〕 练〔練〕 荛〔蕘〕 栉〔櫛〕
诡〔詭〕 组〔組〕 **9 笔** 荜〔蓽〕 柷〔櫳〕
询〔詢〕 驵〔駔〕 **【一】** 茧〔繭〕 栋〔棟〕
诣〔詣〕 绅〔紳〕 贰〔貳〕 荞〔蕎〕 栌〔櫨〕
诤〔諍〕 绅〔紬〕 帮〔幫〕 荟〔薈〕 栎〔櫟〕
该〔該〕 细〔細〕 珑〔瓏〕 荠〔薺〕 栏〔欄〕
详〔詳〕 驶〔駛〕 顸〔頇〕 荡〔蕩〕 柠〔檸〕
诧〔詫〕 驸〔駙〕 赵〔戭〕 垩〔堊〕 柽〔檉〕
诨〔諢〕 驺〔騶〕 垭〔埡〕 荣〔榮〕 树〔樹〕
诩〔詡〕 驹〔駒〕 挜〔掗〕 荤〔葷〕 鸲〔鴝〕
终〔終〕 挝〔撾〕 荥〔滎〕 郦〔酈〕
【乛】 织〔織〕 项〔項〕 荦〔犖〕 咸〔鹹〕
*肃〔肅〕 驷〔駟〕 挞〔撻〕 荧〔熒〕 砖〔磚〕
隶〔隸〕 绉〔縐〕 挟〔挾〕 荨〔蕁〕 砗〔硨〕
*录〔錄〕 驻〔駐〕 挠〔撓〕 胡〔鬍〕 砚〔硯〕
弥〔彌〕 绊〔絆〕 赵〔趙〕 荩〔藎〕 砜〔碸〕
〔瀰〕 驼〔駝〕 贲〔賁〕 荪〔蓀〕 面〔麵〕
陕〔陝〕 绋〔紼〕 挡〔擋〕 荫〔蔭〕 牵〔牽〕
驽〔駑〕 绌〔絀〕 垲〔塏〕 荬〔蕒〕 鸥〔鷗〕
驾〔駕〕 绍〔紹〕 挢〔撟〕 荭〔葒〕 龚〔龔〕
*参〔參〕 驿〔驛〕 垫〔墊〕 荮〔葤〕 残〔殘〕
艰〔艱〕 绎〔繹〕 挤〔擠〕 药〔藥〕 殇〔殤〕
线〔綫〕 经〔經〕 挥〔揮〕 标〔標〕 轱〔軲〕
绀〔紺〕 骀〔駘〕 挦〔撏〕 轲〔軻〕
绁〔紲〕 绐〔紿〕 *荐〔薦〕 轳〔轤〕

29

轴〔軸〕 蚁〔蟻〕 钛〔鈦〕 秋〔鞦〕 狯〔獪〕
轶〔軼〕 蚂〔螞〕 钚〔鈈〕 复〔復〕 狱〔獄〕
轷〔軤〕 虽〔雖〕 钝〔鈍〕 〔複〕 狲〔猻〕
轸〔軫〕 骂〔罵〕 钞〔鈔〕 〔覆〕 贸〔貿〕
轹〔轢〕 哕〔噦〕 钟〔鐘〕 笃〔篤〕 饵〔餌〕
轺〔軺〕 剐〔剮〕 〔鍾〕 俦〔儔〕 饶〔饒〕
轻〔輕〕 郧〔鄖〕 钡〔鋇〕 俨〔儼〕 蚀〔蝕〕
鸦〔鴉〕 勋〔勛〕 钢〔鋼〕 俩〔倆〕 饷〔餉〕
蚤〔蠱〕 哗〔嘩〕 钠〔鈉〕 俪〔儷〕 饸〔餄〕
【丨】 响〔響〕 钥〔鑰〕 贷〔貸〕 饹〔餎〕
战〔戰〕 哙〔噲〕 钦〔欽〕 顺〔順〕 饺〔餃〕
觇〔覘〕 哝〔噥〕 钧〔鈞〕 俭〔儉〕 饻〔餏〕
点〔點〕 哟〔喲〕 铃〔鈴〕 剑〔劍〕 饼〔餅〕
临〔臨〕 峡〔峽〕 钨〔鎢〕 鸧〔鶬〕 【丶】
览〔覽〕 峣〔嶢〕 钩〔鉤〕 须〔須〕 峦〔巒〕
竖〔豎〕 帧〔幀〕 钪〔鈧〕 〔鬚〕 弯〔彎〕
*尝〔嘗〕 罚〔罰〕 钫〔鈁〕 胧〔朧〕 孪〔孿〕
眍〔瞘〕 峤〔嶠〕 钬〔鈥〕 胨〔腖〕 娈〔孌〕
眬〔矓〕 贱〔賤〕 钭〔鈄〕 胪〔臚〕 *将〔將〕
哑〔啞〕 贴〔貼〕 钮〔鈕〕 胆〔膽〕 奖〔獎〕
显〔顯〕 贶〔貺〕 钯〔鈀〕 胜〔勝〕 疬〔癧〕
哒〔噠〕 贻〔貽〕 毡〔氈〕 胫〔脛〕 疮〔瘡〕
哓〔嘵〕 【丿】 氢〔氫〕 鸽〔鴿〕 疯〔瘋〕
哔〔嗶〕 钘〔鈃〕 选〔選〕 狭〔狹〕 *亲〔親〕
贵〔貴〕 钙〔鈣〕 适〔適〕 狮〔獅〕 飒〔颯〕
虾〔蝦〕 钚〔鈈〕 种〔種〕 独〔獨〕 闺〔閨〕

30

闻〔聞〕　浉〔溮〕　诮〔誚〕　绒〔絨〕　珲〔琿〕
阌〔閿〕　浊〔濁〕　祢〔禰〕　结〔結〕　蚕〔蠶〕
闽〔閩〕　测〔測〕　误〔誤〕　绔〔絝〕　顽〔頑〕
间〔間〕　浍〔澮〕　诰〔誥〕　骁〔驍〕　盏〔盞〕
闱〔闈〕　浏〔瀏〕　诱〔誘〕　绕〔繞〕　捞〔撈〕
阀〔閥〕　济〔濟〕　诲〔誨〕　经〔經〕　载〔載〕
阁〔閣〕　浐〔滻〕　诳〔誑〕　骄〔驕〕　赶〔趕〕
闸〔閘〕　浑〔渾〕　鸠〔鳩〕　骅〔驊〕　盐〔鹽〕
阂〔閡〕　浒〔滸〕　说〔說〕　绘〔繪〕　埘〔塒〕
养〔養〕　浓〔濃〕　诵〔誦〕　骆〔駱〕　损〔損〕
姜〔薑〕　浔〔潯〕　诶〔誒〕　骈〔駢〕　埙〔塤〕
类〔類〕　浕〔濜〕　　　　　绞〔絞〕　埚〔堝〕
*娄〔婁〕　恸〔慟〕　【乛】　骇〔駭〕　捡〔撿〕
总〔總〕　恹〔懨〕　垦〔墾〕　统〔統〕　贽〔贄〕
炼〔煉〕　恺〔愷〕　昼〔晝〕　绗〔絎〕　挚〔摯〕
炽〔熾〕　恻〔惻〕　费〔費〕　给〔給〕　热〔熱〕
烁〔爍〕　恼〔惱〕　逊〔遜〕　绚〔絢〕　捣〔搗〕
烂〔爛〕　恽〔惲〕　陨〔隕〕　绛〔絳〕　壶〔壺〕
烃〔烴〕　*举〔舉〕　险〔險〕　络〔絡〕　*聂〔聶〕
洼〔窪〕　觉〔覺〕　贺〔賀〕　绝〔絕〕　莱〔萊〕
洁〔潔〕　宪〔憲〕　怼〔懟〕　　　　　莲〔蓮〕
洒〔灑〕　窃〔竊〕　垒〔壘〕　**10 笔**　莳〔蒔〕
挞〔撻〕　诚〔誠〕　娅〔婭〕　【一】　莴〔萵〕
狭〔狹〕　诬〔誣〕　娆〔嬈〕　艳〔艷〕　获〔獲〕
浇〔澆〕　语〔語〕　娇〔嬌〕　项〔項〕　　〔穫〕
浈〔湞〕　袄〔襖〕　绑〔綁〕　　　　　莸〔蕕〕

31

恶〔惡〕
〔噁〕
劳〔蕣〕
莹〔瑩〕
莺〔鶯〕
鸪〔鴣〕
莼〔蒓〕
桡〔橈〕
桢〔楨〕
档〔檔〕
桤〔榿〕
桥〔橋〕
桦〔樺〕
桧〔檜〕
桩〔樁〕
样〔樣〕
贾〔賈〕
逦〔邐〕
砺〔礪〕
砾〔礫〕
础〔礎〕
砻〔礱〕
顾〔顧〕
轼〔軾〕
轻〔輕〕
轿〔轎〕

辂〔輅〕
较〔較〕
鸫〔鶇〕
顿〔頓〕
趸〔躉〕
毙〔斃〕
致〔緻〕
【丨】
龀〔齔〕
鸬〔鸕〕
*虑〔慮〕
*监〔監〕
紧〔緊〕
*党〔黨〕
唛〔嘜〕
晒〔曬〕
晓〔曉〕
唝〔嗊〕
唠〔嘮〕
鸭〔鴨〕
唡〔啢〕
晔〔曄〕
晕〔暈〕
鸮〔鴞〕
唢〔嗩〕
呙〔喎〕

蚬〔蜆〕
鸯〔鴦〕
崂〔嶗〕
崃〔崍〕
*罢〔罷〕
圆〔圓〕
觊〔覬〕
贼〔賊〕
贿〔賄〕
赂〔賂〕
赃〔臟〕
赅〔賅〕
赆〔贐〕
【丿】
钰〔鈺〕
钱〔錢〕
钲〔鉦〕
钳〔鉗〕
钴〔鈷〕
钵〔缽〕
钶〔鈳〕
钷〔鉕〕
钹〔鈸〕
钺〔鉞〕
钻〔鑽〕
钼〔鉬〕

钽〔鉭〕
钾〔鉀〕
铀〔鈾〕
钿〔鈿〕
铁〔鐵〕
铂〔鉑〕
铃〔鈴〕
铄〔鑠〕
铅〔鉛〕
铆〔鉚〕
铈〔鈰〕
铉〔鉉〕
铊〔鉈〕
铋〔鉍〕
铌〔鈮〕
铍〔鈹〕
铍〔鑔〕
铎〔鐸〕
氢〔氫〕
牺〔犧〕
敌〔敵〕
积〔積〕
称〔稱〕
笕〔筧〕
*笔〔筆〕
债〔債〕

借〔藉〕
倾〔傾〕
赁〔賃〕
顽〔頑〕
徕〔徠〕
舰〔艦〕
舱〔艙〕
耸〔聳〕
*爱〔愛〕
鸰〔鴒〕
颁〔頒〕
颂〔頌〕
脍〔膾〕
脏〔臟〕
〔髒〕
脐〔臍〕
脑〔腦〕
胶〔膠〕
脓〔膿〕
鸱〔鴟〕
玺〔璽〕
刽〔劊〕
鸲〔鴝〕
猃〔獫〕
鸵〔鴕〕
袅〔裊〕

鸳〔鴛〕	烦〔煩〕	窍〔竅〕	剧〔劇〕	麸〔麩〕
皱〔皺〕	烧〔燒〕	窝〔窩〕	娲〔媧〕	掳〔擄〕
馂〔餕〕	烛〔燭〕	请〔請〕	娴〔嫻〕	掴〔摑〕
饿〔餓〕	烨〔燁〕	诸〔諸〕	*难〔難〕	鸷〔鷙〕
馁〔餒〕	烩〔燴〕	诹〔諏〕	预〔預〕	掷〔擲〕
【、】	烬〔燼〕	诺〔諾〕	绠〔綆〕	掸〔撣〕
栾〔欒〕	递〔遞〕	诼〔諑〕	骊〔驪〕	壶〔壺〕
挛〔攣〕	涛〔濤〕	读〔讀〕	骋〔騁〕	悫〔愨〕
恋〔戀〕	涝〔澇〕	诽〔誹〕	绢〔絹〕	据〔據〕
桨〔槳〕	涞〔淶〕	袜〔襪〕	绣〔綉〕	掺〔摻〕
浆〔漿〕	涟〔漣〕	祯〔禎〕	验〔驗〕	掼〔摜〕
症〔癥〕	涠〔潿〕	课〔課〕	绥〔綏〕	职〔職〕
痈〔癰〕	涢〔溳〕	诿〔諉〕	绦〔縧〕	聍〔聹〕
斋〔齋〕	涡〔渦〕	谀〔諛〕	继〔繼〕	萚〔蘀〕
痉〔痙〕	涂〔塗〕	谁〔誰〕	绨〔綈〕	勚〔勩〕
准〔準〕	涤〔滌〕	谂〔諗〕	骎〔駸〕	萝〔蘿〕
*离〔離〕	润〔潤〕	调〔調〕	骏〔駿〕	萤〔螢〕
顽〔頑〕	涧〔澗〕	谄〔諂〕	鸶〔鷥〕	营〔營〕
资〔資〕	涨〔漲〕	谅〔諒〕		萦〔縈〕
竞〔競〕	烫〔燙〕	谆〔諄〕	**11 笔**	萧〔蕭〕
阃〔閫〕	涩〔澀〕	谇〔誶〕		萨〔薩〕
阄〔鬮〕	悭〔慳〕	谈〔談〕	【一】	梦〔夢〕
阅〔閲〕	悯〔憫〕	谊〔誼〕	焘〔燾〕	觋〔覡〕
阆〔閬〕	宽〔寬〕	谞〔譖〕	琎〔璡〕	检〔檢〕
郸〔鄲〕	家〔傢〕	【乛】	琏〔璉〕	棂〔欞〕
	*宾〔賓〕	恳〔懇〕	琐〔瑣〕	*啬〔嗇〕

匦〔匭〕
酝〔醞〕
厣〔厴〕
硕〔碩〕
硖〔硤〕
硗〔磽〕
砲〔礮〕
硚〔礄〕
鸸〔鴯〕
聋〔聾〕
龚〔龔〕
袭〔襲〕
驾〔駕〕
殒〔殞〕
殓〔殮〕
赍〔賫〕
辄〔輒〕
辅〔輔〕
辆〔輛〕
堑〔塹〕
【丨】
颅〔顱〕
啧〔嘖〕
悬〔懸〕
啭〔囀〕
跃〔躍〕

啮〔嚙〕
跄〔蹌〕
蛎〔蠣〕
蛊〔蠱〕
蛏〔蟶〕
累〔纍〕
啸〔嘯〕
帻〔幘〕
崭〔嶄〕
逻〔邏〕
帼〔幗〕
赈〔賑〕
婴〔嬰〕
赊〔賒〕
【丿】
铡〔鍘〕
铐〔銬〕
铑〔銠〕
铒〔鉺〕
铓〔鋩〕
铕〔銪〕
铗〔鋏〕
铙〔鐃〕
铛〔鐺〕
铝〔鋁〕
铜〔銅〕

锦〔錦〕
铟〔銦〕
铠〔鎧〕
铡〔鍘〕
铢〔銖〕
铣〔銑〕
铥〔銩〕
铤〔鋌〕
铧〔鏵〕
铨〔銓〕
铩〔鎩〕
铪〔鉿〕
铫〔銚〕
铭〔銘〕
铬〔鉻〕
铮〔錚〕
铯〔銫〕
铰〔鉸〕
铱〔銥〕
铲〔鏟〕
铳〔銃〕
铵〔銨〕
银〔銀〕
铷〔銣〕
矫〔矯〕
鹄〔鵠〕

秽〔穢〕
笺〔箋〕
笼〔籠〕
笾〔籩〕
偾〔僨〕
鸺〔鵂〕
偿〔償〕
偻〔僂〕
躯〔軀〕
皑〔皚〕
衅〔釁〕
鸼〔鵃〕
衔〔銜〕
舻〔艫〕
盘〔盤〕
鸻〔鴴〕
龛〔龕〕
鸽〔鴿〕
敛〔斂〕
领〔領〕
脶〔腡〕
脸〔臉〕
象〔像〕
猎〔獵〕
猡〔玀〕
猕〔獼〕

馃〔餜〕
馄〔餛〕
馅〔餡〕
馆〔館〕
【丶】
鸾〔鸞〕
庼〔廎〕
痒〔癢〕
鹒〔鶊〕
旋〔鏇〕
阄〔鬮〕
阆〔閬〕
阅〔閱〕
阃〔閫〕
阈〔閾〕
阉〔閹〕
阊〔閶〕
阎〔閻〕
阐〔闡〕
羟〔羥〕
盖〔蓋〕
栌〔櫨〕
*断〔斷〕
兽〔獸〕
焖〔燜〕
渍〔漬〕

鸿〔鴻〕 谒〔謁〕 绪〔緒〕

12 笔

椭〔橢〕
浃〔浹〕 谓〔謂〕 绫〔綾〕 鸽〔鴿〕
渐〔漸〕 谔〔諤〕 骐〔騏〕 **【一】** 鹇〔鷴〕
浘〔潿〕 谕〔諭〕 续〔續〕 靓〔靚〕 觌〔覿〕
渊〔淵〕 谖〔諼〕 绮〔綺〕 琼〔瓊〕 硷〔鹼〕
渔〔漁〕 谗〔讒〕 骑〔騎〕 辇〔輦〕 确〔確〕
淀〔澱〕 谘〔諮〕 绯〔緋〕 鼋〔黿〕 詟〔讋〕
渗〔滲〕 谙〔諳〕 绰〔綽〕 趄〔趄〕 殚〔殫〕
恓〔悽〕 谚〔諺〕 骒〔騍〕 揽〔攬〕 颊〔頰〕
惭〔慚〕 谛〔諦〕 绲〔緄〕 颉〔頡〕 雳〔靂〕
惧〔懼〕 谜〔謎〕 绳〔繩〕 揿〔撳〕 辊〔輥〕
惊〔驚〕 谝〔諞〕 骓〔騅〕 换〔攙〕 辋〔輞〕
惮〔憚〕 谞〔諝〕 维〔維〕 蛰〔蟄〕 椠〔槧〕
惨〔慘〕 **【乛】** 绵〔綿〕 絷〔縶〕 暂〔暫〕
惯〔慣〕 绥〔綏〕 搁〔擱〕 辍〔輟〕
祷〔禱〕 弹〔彈〕 绷〔綳〕 搂〔摟〕 辎〔輜〕
谌〔諶〕 堕〔墮〕 绸〔綢〕 搅〔攪〕 翘〔翹〕
谋〔謀〕 随〔隨〕 绺〔綹〕 联〔聯〕
谍〔諜〕 粜〔糶〕 绻〔綣〕 蒇〔蔵〕 **【丨】**
谎〔謊〕 *隐〔隱〕 综〔綜〕 蒉〔蕢〕 辈〔輩〕
谏〔諫〕 婳〔嫿〕 绽〔綻〕 蒋〔蔣〕 凿〔鑿〕
鞁〔鞁〕 婵〔嬋〕 绾〔綰〕 蒌〔蔞〕 辉〔輝〕
谐〔諧〕 婶〔嬸〕 绿〔綠〕 韩〔韓〕 赏〔賞〕
谑〔謔〕 颇〔頗〕 骖〔驂〕 椟〔櫝〕 睐〔睞〕
裆〔襠〕 颈〔頸〕 缀〔綴〕 椤〔欏〕 睑〔瞼〕
祸〔禍〕 绩〔績〕 缁〔緇〕 赍〔齎〕 喷〔噴〕
畴〔疇〕

35

践〔踐〕	铿〔鏗〕	筚〔篳〕	【丶】	湾〔灣〕
遗〔遺〕	销〔銷〕	筛〔篩〕	亵〔褻〕	谟〔謨〕
蛱〔蛺〕	锁〔鎖〕	牍〔牘〕	装〔裝〕	裢〔褳〕
蛲〔蟯〕	锃〔鋥〕	傥〔儻〕	蛮〔蠻〕	裣〔襝〕
蛳〔螄〕	锄〔鋤〕	傧〔儐〕	脔〔臠〕	裤〔褲〕
蛴〔蠐〕	锂〔鋰〕	储〔儲〕	痨〔癆〕	裥〔襇〕
鹃〔鵑〕	锅〔鍋〕	傩〔儺〕	痫〔癇〕	禅〔禪〕
喽〔嘍〕	锆〔鋯〕	惩〔懲〕	赓〔賡〕	谠〔讜〕
嵘〔嶸〕	锇〔鋨〕	御〔禦〕	颏〔頦〕	谡〔謖〕
嵚〔嶔〕	锈〔銹〕	颌〔頜〕	鹇〔鷳〕	谢〔謝〕
嵝〔嶁〕	锉〔銼〕	释〔釋〕	阑〔闌〕	谣〔謠〕
赋〔賦〕	锋〔鋒〕	鹆〔鵒〕	阒〔闃〕	谤〔謗〕
腈〔腈〕	锌〔鋅〕	腊〔臘〕	阔〔闊〕	谥〔謚〕
赌〔賭〕	锎〔鐦〕	腘〔膕〕	阕〔闋〕	谦〔謙〕
赎〔贖〕	铜〔銅〕	鱿〔魷〕	粪〔糞〕	谧〔謐〕
赐〔賜〕	锐〔銳〕	鲁〔魯〕	鹈〔鵜〕	
赒〔賙〕	锑〔銻〕	鲂〔魴〕	*窜〔竄〕	【乛】
赔〔賠〕	锒〔鋃〕	颍〔潁〕	窝〔窩〕	*属〔屬〕
赕〔賧〕	锓〔鋟〕	飓〔颶〕	謍〔謍〕	屡〔屢〕
【丿】	铜〔鋦〕	觞〔觴〕	愦〔憒〕	骘〔騭〕
铸〔鑄〕	锏〔鐧〕	惫〔憊〕	愤〔憤〕	毹〔毹〕
锛〔錛〕	犊〔犢〕	馇〔餷〕	滞〔滯〕	羟〔羥〕
铺〔鋪〕	鹄〔鵠〕	馈〔饋〕	湿〔濕〕	骛〔騖〕
铼〔錸〕	鹅〔鵝〕	馉〔餶〕	溃〔潰〕	缂〔緙〕
铽〔鋱〕	颊〔頰〕	馊〔餿〕	溅〔濺〕	缃〔緗〕
链〔鏈〕	筑〔築〕	馋〔饞〕	溇〔漊〕	缄〔緘〕

36

缅〔緬〕 骛〔騖〕 碛〔磧〕 赠〔贈〕 穄〔穄〕
缆〔纜〕 摄〔攝〕 碍〔礙〕 【丿】 筹〔籌〕
缇〔緹〕 摅〔攄〕 碜〔磣〕 锗〔鍺〕 签〔簽〕
缈〔緲〕 摆〔擺〕 鹌〔鵪〕 错〔錯〕 〔籤〕
缉〔緝〕 〔襬〕 尴〔尷〕 锘〔鍩〕 简〔簡〕
缊〔縕〕 赪〔赬〕 殡〔殯〕 锚〔錨〕 觎〔覦〕
缌〔緦〕 摈〔擯〕 雾〔霧〕 锛〔錛〕 颔〔頷〕
缎〔緞〕 彀〔彀〕 辏〔輳〕 锝〔鍀〕 腻〔膩〕
缑〔緱〕 摊〔攤〕 辐〔輻〕 锞〔錁〕 鹏〔鵬〕
缓〔緩〕 鹊〔鵲〕 辑〔輯〕 锟〔錕〕 腾〔騰〕
缒〔縋〕 蓝〔藍〕 输〔輸〕 锡〔錫〕 鲅〔鮁〕
缔〔締〕 蓦〔驀〕 【丨】 锢〔錮〕 鲆〔鮃〕
缕〔縷〕 鹋〔鶓〕 频〔頻〕 锣〔鑼〕 鲇〔鮎〕
骗〔騙〕 蓟〔薊〕 龃〔齟〕 锤〔錘〕 鲈〔鱸〕
编〔編〕 蒙〔矇〕 龄〔齡〕 锥〔錐〕 鲊〔鮓〕
缗〔緡〕 〔濛〕 龅〔齙〕 锦〔錦〕 稣〔穌〕
骚〔騷〕 〔懞〕 龆〔齠〕 锁〔鎖〕 鲋〔鮒〕
缘〔緣〕 颐〔頤〕 鉴〔鑒〕 锨〔鍁〕 鲕〔鮞〕
飨〔饗〕 *献〔獻〕 龇〔齜〕 锫〔錇〕 鲍〔鮑〕
　 蓣〔蕷〕 龈〔齦〕 锭〔錠〕 鲅〔鮁〕
13 笔 榄〔欖〕 龉〔齬〕 键〔鍵〕 鲐〔鮐〕
　 槚〔檟〕 踌〔躊〕 锯〔鋸〕 颖〔穎〕
【一】 榇〔櫬〕 跸〔蹕〕 锰〔錳〕 鸽〔鴿〕
耢〔耮〕 榈〔櫚〕 跻〔躋〕 锱〔錙〕 飔〔颸〕
鹉〔鵡〕 楼〔樓〕 跹〔躚〕 辞〔辭〕 飕〔颼〕
鸫〔鶇〕 榉〔櫸〕 蜗〔蝸〕 颓〔頹〕 触〔觸〕
韫〔韞〕 赖〔賴〕 嗳〔噯〕 颔〔頜〕
37

雏〔雛〕　滩〔灘〕　缟〔縞〕　槠〔櫧〕　罴〔羆〕
馈〔餽〕　潆〔瀠〕　缠〔纏〕　酽〔釅〕　赗〔賵〕
馍〔饃〕　慑〔懾〕　缡〔縭〕　酾〔釃〕　罂〔罌〕
馏〔餾〕　誉〔譽〕　缢〔縊〕　酿〔釀〕　赚〔賺〕
馕〔饢〕　鲎〔鱟〕　缣〔縑〕　霁〔霽〕　鹛〔鶥〕
【丶】　骞〔騫〕　缤〔繽〕　愿〔願〕　【丿】
酱〔醬〕　寝〔寢〕　骗〔騙〕　殡〔殯〕　锲〔鍥〕
鹑〔鶉〕　窥〔窺〕　　　　　辕〔轅〕　锴〔鍇〕
瘅〔癉〕　窦〔竇〕　14 笔　辖〔轄〕　锶〔鍶〕
瘆〔瘮〕　谨〔謹〕　【一】　辗〔輾〕　锷〔鍔〕
鹧〔鷓〕　谩〔謾〕　瑷〔璦〕　【丨】　锹〔鍬〕
阉〔閹〕　谪〔謫〕　赘〔贅〕　龇〔齜〕　锸〔鍤〕
阗〔闐〕　谫〔謭〕　觏〔覯〕　龈〔齦〕　锻〔鍛〕
阙〔闕〕　谬〔謬〕　韬〔韜〕　鹗〔鶚〕　锼〔鎪〕
誊〔謄〕　【乛】　綮〔縶〕　颗〔顆〕　锾〔鍰〕
粮〔糧〕　辟〔闢〕　墙〔墻〕　瞒〔瞞〕　锵〔鏘〕
数〔數〕　媛〔嬡〕　撄〔攖〕　暧〔曖〕　镀〔鏷〕
滟〔灧〕　嫔〔嬪〕　蔷〔薔〕　鹘〔鶻〕　镁〔銶〕
溓〔溓〕　缙〔縉〕　蔑〔衊〕　踌〔躊〕　镀〔鍍〕
满〔滿〕　缜〔縝〕　蔹〔蘞〕　踊〔踴〕　镁〔鎂〕
滤〔濾〕　缚〔縛〕　蔺〔藺〕　蜡〔蠟〕　镂〔鏤〕
滥〔濫〕　缛〔縟〕　蔼〔藹〕　蝈〔蟈〕　镃〔鎡〕
滗〔潷〕　辔〔轡〕　鹕〔鶘〕　蝇〔蠅〕　镄〔鐨〕
滦〔灤〕　缝〔縫〕　槚〔檟〕　蝉〔蟬〕　镅〔鎇〕
漓〔灕〕　骝〔騮〕　槛〔檻〕　鹗〔鶚〕　鹜〔鶩〕
滨〔濱〕　缫〔繅〕　槟〔檳〕　嘤〔嚶〕　稳〔穩〕
　　　　　　　　　　　　　　　　　　　箦〔簀〕

筷〔篋〕 鎏〔鰲〕 缨〔纓〕 魇〔魘〕 镏〔鎦〕
箨〔籜〕 鳌〔鰲〕 骢〔驄〕 餍〔饜〕 镐〔鎬〕
箩〔籮〕 糁〔糝〕 缩〔縮〕 霉〔黴〕 镑〔鎊〕
箪〔簞〕 鹚〔鷀〕 缪〔繆〕 辘〔轆〕 镒〔鎰〕
箓〔籙〕 潇〔瀟〕 缫〔繰〕 镓〔鎵〕
箫〔簫〕 潋〔瀲〕 **【丨】** 镔〔鑌〕
舆〔輿〕 潍〔濰〕 **15 笔** 龉〔齬〕 镉〔鎘〕
膑〔臏〕 赛〔賽〕 龊〔齪〕 簀〔簀〕
【一】
鲑〔鮭〕 窭〔窶〕 觑〔覷〕 篓〔簍〕
鲒〔鮚〕 谭〔譚〕 耧〔耬〕 瞒〔瞞〕 鹠〔鷚〕
鲔〔鮪〕 谮〔譖〕 璎〔瓔〕 题〔題〕 鹡〔鶺〕
鲖〔鮦〕 褴〔襤〕 殣〔殣〕 颞〔顳〕 鹢〔鷁〕
鲗〔鰂〕 褛〔褸〕 撵〔攆〕 蹑〔躡〕 鲠〔鯁〕
鲙〔鱠〕 谯〔譙〕 撷〔擷〕 踬〔躓〕 鲡〔鱺〕
鲚〔鱭〕 谰〔讕〕 撺〔攛〕 蹒〔蹣〕 鲢〔鰱〕
鲛〔鮫〕 谱〔譜〕 聩〔聵〕 蝶〔蝶〕 鲣〔鰹〕
鲜〔鮮〕 谲〔譎〕 蝼〔螻〕 鲥〔鰣〕
鲟〔鱘〕 聪〔聰〕 噜〔嚕〕 鲤〔鯉〕
【一丨】
飗〔飀〕 觌〔覿〕 嘱〔囑〕 鲦〔鰷〕
鹃〔鷳〕 鞑〔韃〕 颢〔顥〕 鲧〔鯀〕
谨〔謹〕 嫱〔嬙〕 **【丿】**
馒〔饅〕 骛〔騖〕 靳〔鞽〕 鲩〔鯇〕
【丨】 蕲〔蘄〕 镊〔鑷〕 鲫〔鯽〕
【丶】 缥〔縹〕 赜〔賾〕 镇〔鎮〕 徼〔徼〕
銮〔鑾〕 骠〔驃〕 蕴〔蘊〕 镉〔鎘〕 馔〔饌〕
瘗〔瘞〕 缦〔縵〕 樯〔檣〕 锐〔鑭〕 **【丶】**
瘘〔瘻〕 骝〔騮〕 樱〔櫻〕 镌〔鎸〕
阗〔闐〕 缧〔縲〕 飘〔飄〕 镍〔鎳〕 瘪〔癟〕
靥〔靨〕 镎〔錇〕 瘭〔癟〕

39

瘫〔癱〕　颠〔顛〕　赞〔贊〕　黉〔黌〕　镣〔鐐〕
瘪〔癟〕　橹〔櫓〕　穑〔穡〕　【乛】　镤〔鏷〕
颜〔顏〕　橼〔櫞〕　篮〔籃〕　鹨〔鷚〕　镥〔鑥〕
鹣〔鶼〕　鹥〔鷖〕　篱〔籬〕　颡〔顙〕　镦〔鐓〕
鲨〔鯊〕　赝〔贋〕　鲭〔鯖〕　缰〔繮〕　镧〔鑭〕
澜〔瀾〕　飙〔飆〕　鲮〔鯪〕　缱〔繾〕　镨〔鐠〕
额〔額〕　獴〔獷〕　鲰〔鯫〕　缲〔繰〕　镩〔鑹〕
谳〔讞〕　錾〔鏨〕　鲱〔鯡〕　缳〔繯〕　镪〔鏹〕
褴〔襤〕　辙〔轍〕　鲲〔鯤〕　缴〔繳〕　镫〔鐙〕
谴〔譴〕　辚〔轔〕　鲳〔鯧〕　　　　　簖〔籪〕
鹤〔鶴〕　【丨】　鲵〔鯢〕　**17 笔**　鹪〔鷦〕
谵〔譫〕　齹〔齹〕　鲶〔鯰〕　　　　　鳍〔鰭〕
【乛】　螨〔蟎〕　鲷〔鯛〕　【一】　鲽〔鰈〕
屦〔屨〕　鹦〔鸚〕　鲸〔鯨〕　藓〔蘚〕　鳂〔鰃〕
缥〔縹〕　赠〔贈〕　鲻〔鯔〕　鹩〔鷯〕　鳃〔鰓〕
缭〔繚〕　【丿】　獭〔獺〕　【丨】　鳁〔鰮〕
缮〔繕〕　锗〔鍺〕　【丶】　龋〔齲〕　鳄〔鰐〕
缯〔繒〕　镖〔鏢〕　鹧〔鷓〕　龌〔齷〕　鳅〔鰍〕
　　　　镗〔鏜〕　瘿〔癭〕　瞩〔矚〕　鳆〔鰒〕
16 笔　镘〔鏝〕　瘾〔癮〕　蹒〔蹣〕　鳇〔鰉〕
　　　　锁〔鎖〕　斓〔斕〕　蹑〔躡〕　鳈〔鰁〕
【一】　镛〔鏞〕　辩〔辯〕　蟏〔蠨〕　鳉〔鱂〕
糒〔糒〕　镜〔鏡〕　濑〔瀨〕　啮〔嚙〕　【丶】
撷〔擷〕　镝〔鏑〕　濒〔瀕〕　羁〔羈〕　鹫〔鷲〕
颞〔顳〕　镞〔鏃〕　懒〔懶〕　赡〔贍〕　辫〔辮〕
颟〔顢〕　氇〔氌〕　　　　　【丿】
薮〔藪〕　　　　　　　　　镢〔鐝〕

赢〔贏〕
𬇙〔𣾷〕

【乛】

鹝〔鷊〕
骤〔驟〕

18 笔

【一】

鳌〔鼇〕
鞯〔韉〕
黡〔黶〕

【丨】

[illegible]〔[illegible]〕
颢〔顥〕
鹭〔鷺〕
嚣〔囂〕
髅〔髏〕

【丿】

镬〔鑊〕
镭〔鐳〕
镮〔鐶〕
镯〔鐲〕
镰〔鐮〕
镱〔鐿〕
[illegible]〔[illegible]〕
䲢〔鰧〕
鳍〔鰭〕
鳎〔鰨〕
鳏〔鰥〕
鳑〔鰟〕
鳒〔鰜〕

【丶】

鹯〔鸇〕
鹰〔鷹〕
癞〔癩〕
辗〔輾〕
䜩〔讌〕

【乛】

䴙〔鸊〕

19 笔

【一】

攒〔攢〕
霭〔靄〕

【丨】

鳖〔鱉〕
蹿〔躥〕
巅〔巔〕
髋〔髖〕
髌〔髕〕

【丿】

镲〔鑔〕
籁〔籟〕
鳘〔鰵〕
鳓〔鰳〕
鳔〔鰾〕
鳕〔鱈〕
鳗〔鰻〕
鳙〔鱅〕
鳛〔鰼〕

【丶】

颤〔顫〕
癣〔癬〕
谶〔讖〕

【乛】

骥〔驥〕
缵〔纘〕

20 笔

【一】

瓒〔瓚〕
鬓〔鬢〕
颥〔顬〕

【丨】

鼍〔鼉〕
黩〔黷〕

【丿】

镳〔鑣〕
镴〔鑞〕
臜〔臢〕
鳜〔鱖〕
鳝〔鱔〕
鳞〔鱗〕
鳟〔鱒〕

【乛】

骧〔驤〕

21 笔

颦〔顰〕
躏〔躪〕
鳢〔鱧〕
鳣〔鱣〕
癫〔癲〕
赣〔贛〕
灏〔灝〕

22 笔

鹳〔鸛〕
镶〔鑲〕

23 笔

趱〔趲〕
颧〔顴〕
躜〔躦〕

25 笔

𬬻〔钁〕
馕〔饢〕
戆〔戇〕

Complex Form to Simplified Form

C. 从繁体查简体

7 笔

*〔車〕车
*〔夾〕夹
*〔貝〕贝
*〔見〕见
〔壯〕壮
〔妝〕妆

8 笔

【一】
*〔長〕长
*〔亞〕亚
〔軋〕轧
*〔東〕东
*〔兩〕两
〔協〕协

*〔來〕来
*〔戔〕戋

【丨】
*〔門〕门
*〔岡〕冈

【丿】
*〔侖〕仑
〔兒〕儿

【一】
〔狀〕状
〔糾〕纠

9 笔

【一】
〔剋〕克
〔軌〕轨
〔厙〕厍

*〔頁〕页
〔郟〕郏
〔到〕到
〔勁〕劲

【丨】
〔貞〕贞
〔則〕则
〔閂〕闩
〔迴〕回

【丿】
〔俠〕侠
〔係〕系
〔帛〕帛
〔帥〕帅
〔後〕后
〔釓〕钆
〔釔〕钇

〔負〕负
*〔風〕风

【丶】
〔訂〕订
〔計〕计
〔訃〕讣
〔軍〕军
〔衹〕只

【一】
〔陣〕阵
*〔韋〕韦
〔陝〕陕
〔陘〕陉
〔飛〕飞
〔紆〕纡
〔紅〕红
〔紂〕纣

〔紈〕纨
〔級〕级
〔約〕约
〔紇〕纥
〔紀〕纪
〔紉〕纫

10 笔

【一】
*〔馬〕马
〔挾〕挟
〔貢〕贡
*〔華〕华
〔莢〕荚
〔莖〕茎
〔莧〕苋
〔莊〕庄
〔軒〕轩

42

〔連〕连
〔軔〕轫
〔剗〕刬

【丨】

〔鬥〕斗
*〔時〕时
*〔畢〕毕
〔財〕财
〔覎〕觃
〔閃〕闪
〔唄〕呗
〔員〕员
*〔豈〕岂
〔峽〕峡
〔峴〕岘
〔剛〕刚
〔剮〕剐

【丿】

*〔氣〕气
〔郵〕邮
〔倀〕伥
〔倆〕俩
*〔條〕条
〔們〕们
〔個〕个
〔倫〕伦
〔隻〕只
〔島〕岛
*〔烏〕乌
*〔師〕师
〔徑〕径
〔釘〕钉
〔針〕针
〔釗〕钊
〔釙〕钋
〔釕〕钌
*〔殺〕杀
*〔倉〕仓
〔脅〕胁
〔狹〕狭
〔狽〕狈
*〔芻〕刍

【丶】

〔訐〕讦
〔訌〕讧
〔討〕讨
〔訕〕讪
〔訖〕讫
〔訓〕训
〔這〕这
〔訊〕讯
〔記〕记
〔凍〕冻
〔畝〕亩
〔庫〕库
〔浹〕浃
〔涇〕泾

【乛】

〔書〕书
〔陸〕陆
〔陳〕陈
*〔孫〕孙
*〔陰〕阴
〔務〕务
〔紜〕纭
〔純〕纯
〔紕〕纰
〔紗〕纱
〔納〕纳
〔紝〕纴
〔紛〕纷
〔紙〕纸
〔紋〕纹
〔紡〕纺
〔紖〕纼
〔紐〕纽
〔紓〕纾

11 笔

【一】

〔責〕责
〔現〕现
〔甌〕瓯
〔規〕规
*〔殼〕壳
〔埡〕垭
〔掗〕挜
〔捨〕舍
〔捫〕扪
〔掆〕㧏
〔堝〕埚
〔頂〕顶
〔掄〕抡
*〔執〕执
〔捲〕卷
〔掃〕扫
〔堊〕垩
〔萊〕莱
〔萵〕莴
〔乾〕干
〔梘〕枧
〔軛〕轭
〔斬〕斩
〔軟〕软
*〔專〕专
*〔區〕区
〔堅〕坚
*〔帶〕带
〔厠〕厕
〔硃〕朱
*〔麥〕麦
〔頃〕顷

【丨】

*〔鹵〕卤
〔處〕处
〔敗〕败
〔販〕贩
〔貶〕贬
〔啞〕哑
〔閉〕闭
〔問〕问
*〔婁〕娄
〔啢〕唡
*〔國〕国
〔喎〕㖞
〔帳〕帐
〔崬〕岽

〔峽〕峡　〔覓〕觅　〔啟〕启　〔給〕给　〔葦〕苇

〔崗〕岗　〔飥〕饦　〔視〕视　〔貫〕贯　〔葒〕荭

〔圇〕囵　〔貧〕贫　【ㄱ】　*〔鄉〕乡　〔葤〕荮

*〔過〕过　〔脛〕胫　*〔將〕将　　　　　〔根〕根

【丿】　*〔魚〕鱼　〔晝〕昼　**12 笔**　〔棟〕栋

〔氫〕氢　【丶】　〔張〕张　　　　　〔棧〕栈

*〔動〕动　〔詎〕讵　〔階〕阶　【一】　〔椆〕枫

〔偵〕侦　〔訝〕讶　〔陽〕阳　〔貳〕贰　〔極〕极

〔側〕侧　〔訥〕讷　*〔隊〕队　〔預〕预　〔軲〕轱

〔貨〕货　〔許〕许　〔婭〕娅　*〔堯〕尧　〔軻〕轲

*〔進〕进　〔訛〕讹　〔媧〕娲　〔揀〕拣　〔軸〕轴

〔梟〕枭　〔訢〕䜣　〔婦〕妇　〔馭〕驭　〔軼〕轶

*〔鳥〕鸟　〔訩〕讻　〔習〕习　〔項〕项　〔軒〕轩

〔偉〕伟　〔訟〕讼　*〔參〕参　〔賁〕贲　〔軫〕轸

〔徠〕徕　〔設〕设　〔紺〕绀　〔場〕场　〔軺〕轺

〔術〕术　〔訪〕访　〔紲〕绁　〔揚〕扬　*〔畫〕画

*〔從〕从　〔訣〕诀　〔紱〕绂　〔塊〕块　〔腎〕肾

〔釷〕钍　*〔產〕产　〔組〕组　*〔達〕达　〔棗〕枣

〔釺〕钎　〔牽〕牵　〔紳〕绅　〔報〕报　〔硨〕砗

〔釧〕钏　〔烴〕烃　〔紬〕绸　〔揮〕挥　〔硤〕硖

〔釤〕钐　〔淶〕涞　〔細〕细　〔壺〕壶　〔硯〕砚

〔釣〕钓　〔淺〕浅　〔終〕终　〔惡〕恶　〔殘〕残

〔釩〕钒　〔渦〕涡　〔絆〕绊　〔葉〕叶　*〔雲〕云

〔釹〕钕　〔淪〕沦　〔紼〕绋　〔賈〕贾　【｜】

〔釵〕钗　〔悵〕怅　〔絀〕绌　*〔萬〕万　〔覘〕觇

〔貪〕贪　〔鄆〕郓　〔紹〕绍　〔葷〕荤　〔睏〕困

〔喪〕丧

44

〔貼〕贴　*〔筆〕笔　〔鈄〕钭　〔詐〕诈　〔費〕费

〔覘〕觇　*〔備〕备　〔鈕〕钮　〔訴〕诉　〔違〕违

〔貯〕贮　〔貸〕贷　〔鈀〕钯　〔診〕诊　〔韌〕韧

〔貽〕贻　〔順〕顺　〔傘〕伞　〔詆〕诋　〔隕〕陨

〔闈〕闱　〔傖〕伧　〔爺〕爷　〔詞〕词　〔賀〕贺

〔開〕开　〔傯〕偬　〔創〕创　〔詘〕诎　*〔發〕发

〔閑〕闲　〔傢〕家　〔鈍〕钝　〔詔〕诏　〔綁〕绑

〔間〕间　〔鄔〕邬　〔飪〕饪　〔詒〕诒　〔絨〕绒

〔閔〕闵　〔衆〕众　〔飫〕饫　〔馮〕冯　〔結〕结

〔悶〕闷　〔復〕复　〔飭〕饬　〔痙〕痉　〔絝〕绔

〔貴〕贵　〔須〕须　〔飯〕饭　〔勞〕劳　〔經〕经

〔郵〕郲　〔鈃〕钘　〔飲〕饮　〔湞〕浈　〔絎〕绗

〔勛〕勋　〔鈣〕钙　*〔爲〕为　〔測〕测　〔給〕给

*〔單〕单　〔鈈〕钚　〔脹〕胀　〔湯〕汤　〔絢〕绚

〔喲〕哟　〔鈦〕钛　〔腖〕胨　〔淵〕渊　〔絳〕绛

*〔買〕买　〔鈒〕钑　〔膈〕腘　〔渢〕沨　〔絡〕络

〔剴〕剀　〔鈍〕钝　〔勝〕胜　〔渾〕浑　〔絞〕绞

〔凱〕凯　〔鈔〕钞　*〔猶〕犹　〔愜〕惬　〔統〕统

〔幀〕帧　〔鈉〕钠　〔貿〕贸　〔惻〕恻　〔絕〕绝

〔嵐〕岚　〔鈴〕铃　〔鄒〕邹　〔惲〕恽　〔絲〕丝

〔幃〕帏　〔欽〕钦　【丶】　〔惱〕恼　*〔幾〕几

〔圍〕围　〔鈞〕钧　〔詁〕诂　〔運〕运

【丿】　〔鈎〕钩　〔訶〕诃　〔補〕补　**13 笔**

*〔無〕无　〔鈧〕钪　〔評〕评　〔禍〕祸　【一】

〔氫〕氢　〔鈁〕钫　〔詛〕诅　【乛】

*〔喬〕乔　〔鈥〕钬　〔詞〕诇　*〔尋〕寻　〔項〕项

〔琿〕珲　〔蔭〕荫　〔賅〕赅　〔傳〕传　〔鉚〕铆
〔瑋〕玮　〔蒓〕莼　〔嗎〕吗　〔傴〕伛　〔鈰〕铈
〔頑〕顽　〔楨〕桢　〔嘩〕哗　〔傾〕倾　〔鉉〕铉
〔載〕载　〔楊〕杨　〔嗊〕唝　〔僂〕偻　〔鉈〕铊
〔馱〕驮　*〔嗇〕啬　〔暘〕旸　〔賃〕赁　〔鉍〕铋
〔馴〕驯　〔楓〕枫　〔閘〕闸　〔傷〕伤　〔鈮〕铌
〔馳〕驰　〔軾〕轼　*〔黿〕鼋　〔傭〕佣　〔鈹〕铍
〔塒〕埘　〔輊〕轾　〔暈〕晕　〔裊〕袅　*〔僉〕佥
〔塤〕埙　〔輅〕辂　〔號〕号　〔頎〕颀　*〔會〕会
〔損〕损　〔較〕较　〔園〕园　〔鈺〕钰　〔亂〕乱
〔遠〕远　〔竪〕竖　〔蛺〕蛱　〔鉦〕钲　*〔愛〕爱
〔塏〕垲　〔賈〕贾　〔蜆〕蚬　〔鉗〕钳　〔飾〕饰
〔勢〕势　*〔匯〕汇　*〔農〕农　〔鈷〕钴　〔飽〕饱
〔搶〕抢　〔電〕电　〔嗩〕唢　〔鉢〕钵　〔飼〕饲
〔搗〕捣　〔頓〕顿　〔嗶〕哔　〔鉅〕钜　〔飿〕饳
〔塢〕坞　〔盞〕盏　〔鳴〕鸣　〔鈳〕钶　〔飴〕饴
〔壺〕壶　【丨】　〔嗆〕呛　〔鈸〕钹　〔頒〕颁
*〔聖〕圣　*〔歲〕岁　〔圓〕圆　〔鉞〕钺　〔頌〕颂
〔蓋〕盖　*〔虜〕虏　〔骯〕肮　〔鉬〕钼　〔腸〕肠
〔蓮〕莲　*〔業〕业　【丿】　〔鉭〕钽　〔腫〕肿
〔蒔〕莳　*〔當〕当　〔筧〕笕　〔鉀〕钾　〔腦〕脑
〔蓽〕荜　〔睞〕睐　*〔節〕节　〔鈾〕铀　〔魛〕鱽
〔夢〕梦　〔賍〕赃　*〔與〕与　〔鈿〕钿　〔像〕象
〔蒼〕苍　〔賄〕贿　〔債〕债　〔鉑〕铂　〔獁〕犸
〔幹〕干　〔賂〕赂　〔僅〕仅　〔鈴〕铃　〔鳩〕鸠
〔蓀〕荪　　　　　　　　　　〔鉛〕铅　〔獅〕狮

46

〔猻〕狲

【丶】

〔誆〕诓
〔誄〕诔
〔試〕试
〔註〕诖
〔詩〕诗
〔詰〕诘
〔誇〕夸
〔詼〕诙
〔誠〕诚
〔誅〕诛
〔話〕话
〔誕〕诞
〔詬〕诟
〔詮〕诠
〔詭〕诡
〔詢〕询
〔詣〕诣
〔諍〕诤
〔該〕该
〔詳〕详
〔詫〕诧
〔詡〕诩
〔裏〕里

〔準〕准
〔頗〕颇
〔資〕资
〔羥〕羟
*〔義〕义
〔煉〕炼
〔煩〕烦
〔煬〕炀
〔塋〕茔
〔熒〕荧
〔煒〕炜
〔遞〕递
〔溝〕沟
〔漣〕涟
〔滅〕灭
〔溳〕涢
〔滌〕涤
〔溮〕浉
〔塗〕涂
〔滄〕沧
〔愷〕恺
〔愾〕忾
〔愴〕怆
〔惻〕恻
〔窩〕窝
〔禎〕祯

〔褳〕裢

【一】

*〔肅〕肃
〔裝〕装
〔遜〕逊
〔際〕际
〔媽〕妈
〔預〕预
〔疊〕叠
〔綆〕绠
〔經〕经
〔綃〕绡
〔絹〕绢
〔綉〕绣
〔綏〕绥
〔綈〕绨
〔彙〕汇

14 笔

【一】

〔瑪〕玛
〔璉〕琏
〔瑣〕琐
〔瑲〕玱
〔駁〕驳

〔摶〕抟
〔摳〕抠
〔趙〕赵
〔趕〕赶
〔摟〕搂
〔摑〕掴
〔臺〕台
〔撾〕挝
〔墊〕垫
*〔壽〕寿
〔摺〕折
〔摻〕掺
〔摜〕掼
〔勩〕勚
〔蔞〕蒌
〔蔦〕茑
〔蓯〕苁
〔蔔〕卜
〔蔣〕蒋
〔蕆〕蒇
〔構〕构
〔樺〕桦
〔檔〕档
〔覡〕觋
〔槍〕枪
〔輒〕辄

〔輔〕辅
〔輕〕轻
〔塹〕堑
〔匭〕匦
*〔監〕监
〔緊〕紧
〔厲〕厉
*〔厭〕厌
〔碩〕硕
〔碭〕砀
〔碸〕砜
〔奩〕奁
*〔爾〕尔
〔奪〕夺
〔殞〕殒
〔鳶〕鸢
〔巰〕巯

【丨】

*〔對〕对
〔幣〕币
〔彆〕别
*〔嘗〕尝
〔嘖〕啧
〔曄〕晔
〔夥〕伙

〔賑〕赈　〔圖〕图　〔銓〕铨　【丶】　*〔鄭〕郑
〔賒〕赊　【丿】　〔鉿〕铪　〔誠〕诚　〔燁〕烨
〔嘆〕叹　〔製〕制　〔銚〕铫　〔誣〕诬　〔熗〕炝
〔暢〕畅　〔種〕种　〔銘〕铭　〔語〕语　〔榮〕荣
〔嘜〕唛　〔稱〕称　〔鉻〕铬　〔誚〕诮　〔熒〕荥
〔閨〕闺　〔箋〕笺　〔錚〕铮　〔誤〕误　〔犖〕荦
〔聞〕闻　〔僥〕侥　〔鉬〕铘　〔誥〕诰　〔熒〕荧
〔閩〕闽　〔債〕债　〔鉸〕铰　〔誘〕诱　〔漬〕渍
〔閭〕闾　〔僕〕仆　〔銥〕铱　〔誨〕诲　〔漢〕汉
〔閥〕阀　〔僑〕侨　〔銃〕铳　〔誑〕诳　〔滿〕满
〔閤〕合　〔僞〕伪　〔銨〕铵　〔說〕说　〔漸〕渐
〔閣〕阁　〔銜〕衔　〔銀〕银　〔認〕认　〔漚〕沤
〔閡〕阂　〔銣〕铷　〔鉶〕铷　〔誦〕诵　〔滯〕滞
〔閱〕阅　〔銬〕铐　〔餞〕饯　〔誒〕诶　〔滷〕卤
〔嘔〕呕　〔銠〕铑　〔餌〕饵　*〔廣〕广　〔漊〕溇
〔蝸〕蜗　〔鉺〕铒　〔蝕〕蚀　〔麼〕么　〔漁〕渔
〔團〕团　〔鎧〕铠　〔餉〕饷　〔廎〕庼　〔滸〕浒
〔嘍〕喽　〔銷〕销　〔餄〕饸　〔瘖〕疟　〔滻〕浐
〔鄲〕郸　〔鋁〕铝　〔餎〕饹　〔瘍〕疡　〔滬〕沪
〔鳴〕鸣　〔銅〕铜　〔餃〕饺　〔瘋〕疯　〔漲〕涨
〔幘〕帻　〔錦〕锦　〔餏〕饻　〔塵〕尘　〔滲〕渗
〔嶄〕崭　〔銦〕铟　〔餅〕饼　〔颯〕飒　〔慚〕惭
〔嶇〕岖　〔銖〕铢　〔領〕领　〔適〕适　〔慪〕怄
〔罰〕罚　〔銑〕铣　〔鳳〕凤　*〔齊〕齐　〔慳〕悭
〔嶁〕嵝　〔鋋〕铦　〔颱〕台　〔養〕养　〔慟〕恸
〔幗〕帼　〔鋌〕铤　〔獄〕狱　〔鄰〕邻　〔慘〕惨

48

〔慣〕惯　〔緋〕绯　〔輦〕辇　〔撏〕挦　〔暫〕暂
〔寬〕宽　〔綽〕绰　〔髮〕发　〔撥〕拨　〔輪〕轮
*〔賓〕宾　〔緄〕绲　〔撓〕挠　〔蕘〕荛　〔輟〕辍
〔窪〕洼　〔綱〕纲　〔墳〕坟　〔蕆〕蒇　〔輜〕辎
*〔寧〕宁　〔網〕网　〔撻〕挞　〔蕓〕芸　〔甌〕瓯
〔寢〕寝　〔維〕维　〔駔〕驵　〔邁〕迈　〔歐〕欧
〔實〕实　〔綿〕绵　〔駛〕驶　〔蕢〕蒉　〔毆〕殴
〔皸〕皲　〔綸〕纶　〔駟〕驷　〔蕒〕荬　〔賢〕贤
〔複〕复　〔綏〕绥　〔駙〕驸　〔蕪〕芜　*〔遷〕迁

【一】　〔綳〕绷　〔駒〕驹　〔蕎〕荞　〔鴆〕鸩
〔劃〕划　〔綢〕绸　〔駐〕驻　〔蕕〕莸　〔憂〕忧
*〔盡〕尽　〔綹〕绺　〔駝〕驼　〔蕩〕荡　〔碼〕码
〔屢〕屡　〔綣〕卷　〔駘〕骀　〔蕁〕荨　〔磴〕砘
〔獎〕奖　〔綜〕综　〔撲〕扑　〔樁〕桩　〔確〕确
〔墮〕堕　〔綻〕绽　〔頡〕颉　〔樞〕枢　〔賫〕赍
〔隨〕随　〔縮〕缩　〔撣〕掸　〔標〕标　〔遼〕辽
〔載〕载　〔綠〕绿　*〔賣〕卖　〔樓〕楼　〔殤〕殇
〔墜〕坠　〔綴〕缀　〔撫〕抚　〔樅〕枞　〔鴉〕鸦
〔嫗〕妪　〔緇〕缁　〔撟〕挢

〔頗〕颇　　　　　〔撳〕揿　〔賚〕赉　【丨】
〔態〕态　**15 笔**　〔熱〕热　〔樣〕样　〔輩〕辈
〔鄧〕邓　　　　　〔鞏〕巩　〔橢〕椭　〔劌〕刿
〔緒〕绪　【一】　〔摯〕挚　〔輛〕辆　*〔齒〕齿
〔綾〕绫　〔鬧〕闹　〔撈〕捞　〔輥〕辊　〔劇〕剧
〔綺〕绮　〔璡〕琎　〔穀〕谷　〔輞〕辋　〔膚〕肤
〔綫〕线　〔靚〕靓　〔慤〕悫　〔槧〕椠　*〔慮〕虑
　　　　　　　　　　　　　　　　　〔鄴〕邺

49

〔輝〕辉　〔嘰〕叽　〔鋪〕铺　〔餘〕余　〔調〕调
〔賞〕赏　〔嶢〕峣　〔鋏〕铗　〔餒〕馁　〔諂〕谄
〔賦〕赋　*〔罷〕罢　〔鉽〕铽　〔膞〕䏝　〔諒〕谅
〔睛〕晴　〔嶠〕峤　〔銷〕销　〔膃〕䐃　〔諄〕谆
〔賬〕账　〔嶔〕嵚　〔鋥〕锃　〔膠〕胶　〔誶〕谇
〔賭〕赌　〔幟〕帜　〔鋰〕锂　〔鵃〕鸼　〔談〕谈
〔賤〕贱　〔嶗〕崂　〔鋇〕钡　〔魷〕鱿　〔誼〕谊
〔賜〕赐　【丿】　〔鋤〕锄　〔魯〕鲁　〔廟〕庙
〔賙〕赒　〔頍〕颏　〔鋯〕锆　〔魴〕鲂　〔廠〕厂
〔賠〕赔　〔篋〕箧　〔鋨〕锇　〔穎〕颖　〔廡〕庑
〔賒〕赊　〔範〕范　〔銹〕锈　〔颾〕刮　〔瘞〕瘗
〔嶢〕哓　〔價〕价　〔銼〕锉　*〔劉〕刘　〔瘡〕疮
〔噴〕喷　〔儂〕侬　〔鋒〕锋　〔皺〕皱　〔賡〕赓
〔噠〕哒　〔儉〕俭　〔鋅〕锌　【丶】　〔慶〕庆
〔噁〕恶　〔儈〕侩　〔銳〕锐　〔請〕请　〔廢〕废
〔闔〕阖　〔億〕亿　〔銻〕锑　〔諸〕诸　〔敵〕敌
〔闖〕闯　〔儀〕仪　〔鋃〕锒　〔諏〕诹　〔頜〕颌
〔閱〕阅　〔皚〕皑　〔鋄〕锓　〔諑〕诼　〔導〕导
〔闐〕阗　*〔樂〕乐　〔鋼〕钢　〔誹〕诽　〔瑩〕莹
〔數〕数　*〔質〕质　〔鍋〕锅　〔課〕课　〔潔〕洁
〔踐〕践　〔徵〕征　〔領〕领　〔諉〕诿　〔澆〕浇
〔遺〕遗　〔衝〕冲　〔劍〕剑　〔諛〕谀　〔澾〕挞
〔蝦〕虾　〔慫〕怂　〔劊〕刽　〔誰〕谁　〔潤〕润
〔嘸〕呒　〔徹〕彻　〔鄶〕郐　〔論〕论　〔澗〕涧
〔嘮〕唠　〔衛〕卫　〔鋕〕铩　〔餓〕饿　〔潰〕溃
〔嗦〕咝　〔盤〕盘　〔餓〕饿　〔諗〕谂　〔澠〕渑

50

〔潭〕滗 〔嫻〕娴 〔緝〕缉 〔蕭〕萧 〔殨〕㱮
〔潙〕沩 〔駕〕驾 〔緯〕纬 〔頤〕颐 〔殫〕殚
〔澇〕涝 〔嬋〕婵 〔縁〕缘 〔鴣〕鸪 〔頸〕颈
〔潯〕浔 〔嫵〕妩 〔薩〕萨
〔潑〕泼 〔嬌〕娇 **16 笔** 〔蕷〕蓣 【丨】
〔憒〕愦 〔嫿〕妫 〔橈〕桡 〔頻〕频
〔憫〕悯 〔嬭〕嬭 【一】 〔樹〕树 *〔盧〕卢
〔憒〕愦 〔駑〕驽 〔璣〕玑 〔樸〕朴 〔曉〕晓
〔憚〕惮 〔翬〕翚 〔墙〕墙 〔橋〕桥 〔瞞〕瞒
〔憮〕怃 〔氄〕氄 〔駱〕骆 〔機〕机 〔縣〕县
〔憐〕怜 〔緯〕缂 〔駭〕骇 〔轅〕辕 〔瞘〕眍
*〔寫〕写 〔緗〕缃 〔駢〕骈 〔輻〕辐 〔瞜〕䁖
*〔審〕审 〔練〕练 〔擓〕㧟 〔輯〕辑 〔賵〕赗
*〔窮〕穷 〔緘〕缄 〔擄〕掳 〔輸〕输 〔鴨〕鸭
〔褳〕裢 〔緬〕缅 〔擋〕挡 〔賴〕赖 〔閾〕阈
〔褲〕裤 〔緹〕缇 〔擇〕择 〔頭〕头 〔閹〕阉
〔鳩〕鸠 〔緲〕缈 〔赬〕赪 〔醖〕酝 〔閶〕阊
【一】 〔緝〕缉 〔撿〕捡 〔醜〕丑 〔閿〕阌
〔遲〕迟 〔緼〕缊 〔擔〕担 〔勵〕励 〔閣〕阁
〔層〕层 〔緦〕缌 〔壇〕坛 〔磧〕碛 〔閡〕阂
〔彈〕弹 〔緞〕缎 〔擁〕拥 〔磚〕砖 〔閣〕阁
〔選〕选 〔緱〕缑 〔據〕据 〔磣〕碜 〔閱〕阅
〔槳〕桨 〔緇〕缁 〔薔〕蔷 *〔歷〕历 〔曇〕昙
〔漿〕浆 〔緩〕缓 〔薑〕姜 〔曆〕历 〔噸〕吨
〔險〕险 〔締〕缔 〔薈〕荟 〔奮〕奋 〔鴞〕鸮
〔嬈〕娆 〔編〕编 〔薊〕蓟 〔頰〕颊 〔噯〕哎
*〔薦〕荐 〔頰〕颊 〔踴〕踊

51

〔螞〕蚂	〔懕〕恿	〔錇〕锫	〔鮍〕鲏	〔諦〕谛
〔蛳〕蛳	〔儕〕侪	〔錠〕锭	〔鮊〕鲌	〔謎〕谜
〔噹〕当	〔儐〕傧	〔鍵〕键	〔鮐〕鲐	〔諢〕诨
〔駡〕骂	〔儘〕尽	*〔録〕录	〔鴝〕鸲	〔諞〕谝
〔噥〕哝	〔鴕〕鸵	〔鋸〕锯	〔獲〕获	〔諱〕讳
〔戰〕战	〔艙〕舱	〔錳〕锰	〔穎〕颖	〔諝〕谞
〔噲〕哙	〔錶〕表	〔錙〕锱	〔獨〕独	〔憑〕凭
〔鴦〕鸯	〔鍺〕锗	〔覦〕觎	〔獫〕猃	〔鄺〕邝
〔噯〕嗳	〔錯〕错	〔墾〕垦	〔獪〕狯	〔瘻〕瘘
〔嘯〕啸	〔鍩〕锘	〔餞〕饯	〔駕〕驾	〔瘮〕瘆
〔還〕还	〔錨〕锚	〔餜〕馃	【丶】	*〔親〕亲
〔嶧〕峄	〔錛〕锛	〔餛〕馄	〔謀〕谋	〔辦〕办
〔嶼〕屿	〔錸〕铼	〔餡〕馅	〔諶〕谌	*〔龍〕龙
【丿】	〔錢〕钱	〔館〕馆	〔諜〕谍	〔劑〕剂
〔積〕积	〔鍀〕锝	〔頷〕颔	〔謊〕谎	〔燒〕烧
〔頰〕颊	〔錁〕锞	〔鴿〕鸽	〔諫〕谏	〔燜〕焖
〔穆〕穆	〔錕〕锟	〔膩〕腻	〔諧〕谐	〔熾〕炽
〔篤〕笃	〔釘〕钉	〔鴎〕鸥	〔謔〕谑	〔螢〕萤
〔築〕筑	〔錫〕锡	〔鮁〕鲅	〔謁〕谒	〔營〕营
〔篳〕筚	〔錮〕锢	〔鮃〕鲆	〔謂〕谓	〔縈〕萦
〔篩〕筛	〔鋼〕钢	〔鮎〕鲇	〔諤〕谔	〔燈〕灯
*〔舉〕举	〔鍋〕锅	〔鮓〕鲊	〔諭〕谕	〔濛〕蒙
〔興〕兴	〔錘〕锤	〔穌〕稣	〔諼〕谖	〔燙〕烫
〔嶜〕峃	〔錐〕锥	〔鮒〕鲋	〔諷〕讽	〔澠〕渑
〔學〕学	〔錦〕锦	〔鯽〕鲫	〔諮〕谘	〔濃〕浓
〔儔〕俦	〔鍁〕锨	〔鮑〕鲍	〔諺〕谚	〔澤〕泽

52

〔濁〕浊　〔縞〕缟　〔擯〕摈　〔臨〕临　〔闈〕闱
〔澮〕浍　〔縭〕缡　〔撑〕拧　〔磽〕硗　〔闋〕闵
〔澱〕淀　〔縑〕缣　〔轂〕毂　〔壓〕压　〔暧〕暖
〔涳〕涞　〔縊〕缢　〔聲〕声　〔礄〕硚　〔蹕〕跸
〔懞〕蒙　　　　　〔藉〕借　〔磯〕矶　〔蹌〕跄
〔懌〕怿　**17 笔**　〔聰〕聪　〔鴯〕鸸　〔螞〕蚂
〔憶〕忆　　　　　〔聯〕联　〔邇〕迩　〔螻〕蝼
〔憲〕宪　【一】　〔艱〕艰　〔艦〕舰　〔蟈〕蝈
〔窺〕窥　〔樓〕楼　〔藍〕蓝　〔鴷〕䴕　〔雖〕虽
〔寱〕寱　〔環〕环　〔舊〕旧　〔殮〕殓　〔嚀〕咛
〔寫〕写　〔贅〕赘　〔薺〕荠　【丨】　〔覬〕觊
〔褸〕褛　〔璦〕瑷　〔薑〕苤　〔齔〕龀　〔嶺〕岭
〔禪〕禅　〔靚〕靓　〔韓〕韩　〔戲〕戏　〔嶸〕嵘
【乛】　〔黿〕鼋　〔隸〕隶　〔虧〕亏　〔點〕点
*〔隱〕隐　〔幫〕帮　〔桱〕桱　〔斃〕毙　【丿】
〔嬙〕嫱　〔騁〕骋　〔檣〕樯　〔瞭〕了　〔矯〕矫
〔嬡〕嫒　〔駸〕骎　〔檟〕槚　〔顆〕颗　〔鴰〕鸹
〔縉〕缙　〔駿〕骏　〔檔〕档　〔購〕购　〔簀〕箦
〔縝〕缜　〔趨〕趋　〔櫛〕栉　〔賻〕赙　〔簍〕篓
〔縛〕缚　〔擱〕搁　〔檢〕检　〔嬰〕婴　〔輿〕舆
〔縟〕缛　〔擬〕拟　〔檜〕桧　〔賺〕赚　〔歟〕欤
〔緻〕致　〔擴〕扩　〔麯〕曲　〔嚇〕吓　〔鵂〕鸺
〔繿〕绦　〔壙〕圹　〔轅〕辕　〔闌〕阑　*〔龜〕龟
〔縫〕缝　〔擠〕挤　〔轄〕辖　〔闃〕阒　〔優〕优
〔縐〕绉　〔蟄〕蛰　〔輾〕辗　〔闊〕板　〔償〕偿
〔繈〕缥　〔擲〕掷　〔擊〕击　〔闊〕阔　〔儲〕储

53

〔鰤〕鲥
〔鴿〕鸽
〔禦〕御
〔聳〕耸
〔鵃〕鸼
〔鍥〕锲
〔鍇〕锴
〔鍘〕铡
〔錫〕钖
〔鍶〕锶
〔鍔〕锷
〔鍤〕锸
〔鍾〕钟
〔鍛〕锻
〔鎪〕锼
〔鍬〕锹
〔鍰〕锾
〔鎄〕锿
〔鍍〕镀
〔鎂〕镁
〔鎡〕镃
〔鎇〕镅
〔懇〕恳
〔餷〕馇
〔餳〕饧
〔餶〕馉
〔餿〕馊
〔斂〕敛
〔鴿〕鸽
〔膿〕脓
〔臉〕脸
〔膾〕脍
〔膽〕胆
〔謄〕誊
〔鮭〕鲑
〔鮚〕鲒
〔鮪〕鲔
〔鮦〕鲖
〔鮫〕鲛
〔鮮〕鲜
〔颶〕飓
〔獷〕犷
〔獰〕狞

【、】

〔講〕讲
〔謨〕谟
〔謖〕谡
〔謝〕谢
〔謠〕谣
〔謅〕诌
〔謗〕谤
〔謚〕谥
〔謙〕谦
〔謐〕谧
〔褻〕亵
〔氈〕毡
〔應〕应
〔癘〕疠
〔療〕疗
〔癇〕痫
〔癉〕瘅
〔癆〕痨
〔鵁〕䴔
〔齋〕斋
〔鯗〕鲞
〔鯗〕鲞
〔糞〕粪
〔糝〕糁
〔燦〕灿
〔燭〕烛
〔燴〕烩
〔鴻〕鸿
〔濤〕涛
〔濫〕滥
〔濕〕湿
〔濟〕济
〔濱〕滨
〔濘〕泞
〔濜〕浕
〔澀〕涩
〔濰〕潍
〔懨〕恹
〔賽〕赛
〔襇〕裥
〔襀〕䙌
〔襖〕袄
〔禮〕礼

【乛】

〔屨〕屦
〔彌〕弥
〔嬪〕嫔
〔績〕绩
〔縹〕缥
〔縷〕缕
〔縵〕缦
〔縲〕缧
〔總〕总
〔縱〕纵
〔縴〕纤
〔縮〕缩
〔繆〕缪
〔繅〕缫
〔嚮〕向

18 笔

【一】

〔耮〕耢
〔鬩〕阋
〔瓊〕琼
〔攆〕撵
〔鬆〕松
〔翹〕翘
〔擷〕撷
〔擾〕扰
〔騏〕骐
〔騎〕骑
〔騍〕骒
〔騅〕骓
〔攄〕摅
〔擻〕擞
〔鼕〕冬
〔擺〕摆
〔贄〕贽
〔燾〕焘
*〔聶〕聂
〔聵〕聩
〔職〕职
*〔藝〕艺
〔覲〕觐

〔鞦〕秋	〔叢〕丛	〔穡〕穑	〔鴿〕鸽	〔雜〕杂
〔藪〕薮	〔矇〕蒙	〔穢〕秽	〔饃〕馍	*〔離〕离
〔蠆〕虿	〔題〕题	〔簡〕简	〔餺〕馎	〔顏〕颜
〔繭〕茧	〔韙〕韪	〔簣〕篑	〔餼〕饩	〔糧〕粮
〔藥〕药	〔臉〕脸	〔簞〕箪	〔餾〕馏	〔燼〕烬
〔蕘〕荛	〔闊〕阔	*〔雙〕双	〔饊〕馓	〔鵜〕鹈
〔贖〕赎	〔闔〕阖	〔軀〕躯	〔臍〕脐	〔漬〕渍
〔蘊〕蕴	〔闐〕阗	*〔邊〕边	〔鯁〕鲠	〔瀆〕渎
〔檯〕台	〔闖〕闯	*〔歸〕归	〔鯉〕鲤	〔濾〕滤
〔櫃〕柜	〔闕〕阙	〔鏵〕铧	〔鯀〕鲧	〔鯊〕鲨
〔檻〕槛	〔顳〕颞	〔鎮〕镇	〔鯇〕鲩	〔濺〕溅
〔檮〕桐	〔曠〕旷	〔鏈〕链	〔鯽〕鲫	〔瀏〕浏
〔檳〕槟	〔蹣〕蹒	〔鎘〕镉	〔颶〕飓	〔濼〕泺
〔檸〕柠	〔嚙〕啮	〔鎖〕锁	〔颼〕飕	〔瀉〕泻
〔鵓〕鹁	〔壘〕垒	〔鎧〕铠	〔觴〕觞	〔瀋〕沈
〔轉〕转	〔蟯〕蛲	〔鐒〕镃	〔獵〕猎	*〔竄〕窜
〔轆〕辘	*〔蟲〕虫	〔鎳〕镍	〔雛〕雏	〔竅〕窍
〔覆〕复	〔蟬〕蝉	〔鎢〕钨	〔臏〕膑	〔額〕额
〔醫〕医	〔蟣〕虮	〔鍛〕铼	【丶】	〔襧〕袮
〔礎〕础	〔鵑〕鹃	〔錚〕铮	〔謹〕谨	〔襠〕裆
〔殯〕殡	〔嚕〕噜	〔鎦〕镏	〔謳〕讴	〔襝〕裣
〔霧〕雾	〔顓〕颛	〔鎬〕镐	〔謾〕谩	〔禱〕祷
【丨】	【丿】	〔鎊〕镑	〔謫〕谪	【一】
*〔豐〕丰	〔鵠〕鹄	〔鎰〕镒	〔謬〕谬	〔醬〕酱
〔覷〕觑	〔鵝〕鹅	〔鎵〕镓	〔癤〕疖	〔醞〕酝
〔懟〕怼	〔穫〕获	〔鎬〕锔		〔隴〕陇

〔嬸〕婶	〔藺〕蔺	〔鶴〕鹤	〔簫〕箫	〔鯤〕鲲
〔繞〕绕	〔蘺〕蓠	〔璽〕玺	〔犢〕犊	〔鯧〕鲳
〔繚〕缭	〔蘄〕蕲	〔獷〕犷	〔懲〕惩	〔鯢〕鲵
〔織〕织	〔勸〕劝	【丨】	〔鐯〕锗	〔鯰〕鲶
〔繕〕缮	〔蘇〕苏	〔贈〕赠	〔鏗〕铿	〔鯛〕鲷
〔繒〕缯	〔藹〕蔼	〔闔〕阖	〔鏢〕镖	〔鯨〕鲸
*〔斷〕断	〔蘢〕茏	〔關〕关	〔鏜〕镗	〔鯔〕鲻

19 笔

【一】

〔鵡〕鹉	〔顛〕颠	〔嚦〕呖	〔鏤〕镂	〔獺〕獭
〔鶪〕鹃	〔櫝〕椟	〔疇〕畴	〔鏝〕镘	〔鴿〕鸽
〔鬍〕胡	〔櫟〕栎	〔蹺〕跷	〔鏰〕镚	〔颶〕飓
〔騙〕骗	〔櫓〕橹	〔蟶〕蛏	〔鏞〕镛	【丶】
〔騷〕骚	〔櫧〕槠	〔蠅〕蝇	〔鏡〕镜	〔譚〕谭
〔壢〕坜	〔櫞〕橼	〔蟻〕蚁	〔鏟〕铲	〔譖〕潛
〔壚〕垆	〔轎〕轿	*〔嚴〕严	〔鏑〕镝	〔譙〕谯
〔壞〕坏	〔鏨〕錾	〔獸〕兽	〔鏃〕镞	〔識〕识
〔攏〕拢	〔轍〕辙	〔嚨〕咙	〔鏇〕旋	〔譜〕谱
〔擇〕择	〔轔〕辚	〔羆〕罴	〔鏘〕锵	〔證〕证
*〔難〕难	〔繫〕系	*〔羅〕罗	〔辭〕辞	〔譎〕谲
〔鵲〕鹊	〔鶇〕鸫	【丿】	〔饉〕馑	〔譏〕讥
〔藶〕苈	*〔麗〕丽	〔氌〕氇	〔饅〕馒	〔鶉〕鹑
〔蘋〕苹	〔厴〕厣	〔牘〕牍	〔鵬〕鹏	〔廬〕庐
〔蘆〕芦	〔礪〕砺	〔贊〕赞	〔臘〕腊	〔癟〕瘪
〔鵰〕鹛	〔礙〕碍	〔穩〕稳	〔鯖〕鲭	〔癢〕痒
	〔礦〕矿	〔簽〕签	〔鯪〕鲮	〔龐〕庞
	〔贋〕赝	〔簾〕帘	〔鯫〕鲰	〔壟〕垄
	〔願〕愿		〔鯡〕鲱	〔鷳〕鹇

〔類〕类
〔爍〕烁
〔瀟〕潇
〔瀨〕濑
〔瀝〕沥
〔瀕〕濒
〔瀘〕泸
〔瀧〕泷
〔懶〕懒
〔懷〕怀
〔寵〕宠
〔襪〕袜
〔襤〕褴

【一】

〔韜〕韬
〔騖〕骛
〔鶩〕鹜
〔穎〕颖
〔繮〕缰
〔繩〕绳
〔繾〕缱
〔繰〕缲
〔繹〕绎
〔繯〕缳
〔繳〕缴
〔繪〕绘

20 笔

【一】

〔瓏〕珑
〔驁〕骜
〔驊〕骅
〔騮〕骝
〔騶〕驺
〔騙〕骗
〔攖〕撄
〔攔〕拦
〔攙〕搀
〔薴〕苧
〔顢〕颟
〔驀〕蓦
〔蘭〕兰
〔蔽〕荻
〔蘚〕藓
〔鶘〕鹕
〔飄〕飘
〔檽〕栎
〔櫨〕栌
〔櫸〕榉
〔礬〕矾
〔麵〕面
〔櫬〕榇

【丨】

〔鹹〕咸
〔齟〕龃
〔齟〕龃
〔齡〕龄
〔齣〕出
〔齙〕龅
〔齠〕龆
*〔獻〕献
*〔黨〕党
〔懸〕悬
〔鶪〕䴗
〔罌〕罂
〔贍〕赡
〔闥〕闼
〔闡〕阐
〔鶡〕鹖
〔曨〕昽
〔蠣〕蛎
〔躋〕跻
〔蠑〕蝾
〔嚶〕嘤
〔鶚〕鹗
〔髏〕髅

〔鶻〕鹘

【丿】

〔犧〕牺
〔鶩〕鹙
〔籌〕筹
〔籃〕篮
〔譽〕誉
〔覺〕觉
〔譽〕誉
〔巇〕蔹
〔艦〕舰
〔鐃〕铙
〔鏺〕镢
〔鐐〕镣
〔鏷〕镤
〔鐝〕镢
〔鐦〕锎
〔鏷〕镦
〔鐘〕钟
〔鐥〕镨
〔鐥〕锗
〔鐒〕铹
〔鐙〕镫
〔鐝〕钺
〔鐦〕锎
〔鐙〕镫
〔鏺〕钹

【丶】

〔釋〕释
〔饒〕饶
〔儌〕儌
〔饋〕馈
〔饌〕馔
〔饑〕饥
〔臚〕胪
〔朧〕胧
〔騰〕腾
〔鰭〕鳍
〔鰈〕鲽
〔鯛〕鲷
〔鰮〕鳁
〔鰓〕鳃
〔鰐〕鳄
〔鰍〕鳅
〔鰒〕鳆
〔鰉〕鳇
〔鰌〕鳛
〔鯿〕鳊
〔獼〕猕
〔觸〕触

【丶】

〔護〕护
〔譴〕谴
〔譯〕译

57

〔譫〕谵 〔響〕响 【丨】 〔鐳〕镭 〔辯〕辩
〔議〕议 〔齜〕龇 〔鐺〕铛 〔礱〕砻
〔癥〕症 **21 笔** 〔齦〕龈 〔鐸〕铎 〔鶼〕鹣
〔辮〕辫 【一】 〔齪〕龊 〔鐶〕镮 〔爛〕烂
〔襲〕袭 〔糶〕粜 〔贐〕赆 〔鐲〕镯 〔鶯〕莺
〔競〕竞 〔瓔〕璎 〔囁〕嗫 〔鐮〕镰 〔灄〕滠
〔贏〕赢 〔鰲〕鳌 〔囈〕呓 〔鐿〕镱 〔灃〕沣
〔糲〕粝 〔攝〕摄 〔闢〕辟 〔鷳〕鹇 〔灕〕漓
〔糰〕团 〔驟〕骤 〔囀〕啭 〔鷗〕鸥 〔懾〕慑
〔鶿〕鹚 〔驅〕驱 〔顥〕颢 〔鷄〕鸡 〔懼〕惧
〔爐〕炉 〔驃〕骠 〔躊〕踌 〔臢〕臜 〔竈〕灶
〔瀾〕澜 〔驄〕骢 〔躋〕跻 〔騰〕腾 〔顧〕顾
〔瀲〕潋 〔驗〕验 〔躑〕踯 〔鰭〕鳍 〔襯〕衬
〔瀰〕弥 〔攛〕撺 〔躍〕跃 〔鰱〕鲢 〔鶴〕鹤
〔懺〕忏 〔攙〕搀 〔纍〕累 〔鮒〕鲋 【乛】
〔寶〕宝 〔韃〕鞑 〔蠟〕蜡 〔鰷〕鲦 *〔屬〕属
〔騫〕骞 〔韉〕鞯 〔囂〕嚣 〔鰟〕鳑 〔纈〕缬
〔竇〕窦 〔歡〕欢 〔巋〕岿 〔鰜〕鳒 〔續〕续
〔襬〕摆 〔權〕权 〔髒〕脏 〔鰳〕鲏 〔纏〕缠
【乛】 〔櫻〕樱 【丿】 〔鱍〕鲅
〔鶹〕鹠 〔欄〕栏 〔儺〕傩 〔鰜〕鳒 **22 笔**
〔鷙〕鸷 〔轟〕轰 〔儷〕俪 【丶】 【一】
〔纊〕纩 〔覽〕览 〔儼〕俨 〔癲〕癫 〔鬚〕须
〔繽〕缤 〔酈〕郦 〔鷯〕鹩 〔癟〕瘪 〔驍〕骁
〔繼〕继 〔飆〕飙 〔鐵〕铁 〔癮〕瘾 〔驕〕骄
〔饗〕飨 〔殲〕歼 〔鑲〕镶 〔斕〕斓 〔攤〕摊

〔覿〕觌　〔體〕体　〔讅〕谉　〔轤〕轳　〔鱔〕鳝

〔攢〕攒　【丿】　〔戀〕恋　〔靨〕靥　〔鱗〕鳞

〔鷥〕鸶　〔罎〕坛　〔彎〕弯　〔魘〕魇　〔鱒〕鳟

〔聽〕听　〔籜〕箨　〔攣〕挛　〔饜〕餍　〔鱘〕鲟

〔蘿〕萝　〔籟〕籁　〔變〕变　〔鷯〕鹩　【丶】

〔驚〕惊　〔籙〕箓　〔顫〕颤　〔齲〕龋　〔讌〕谳

〔轢〕轹　〔籠〕笼　〔鷓〕鹧　〔顬〕颥　〔欒〕栾

〔鷗〕鸥　〔鱉〕鳖　〔癭〕瘿　【丨】　〔攣〕挛

〔鑒〕鉴　〔儻〕傥　〔癬〕癣　〔曬〕晒　〔變〕变

〔邐〕逦　〔艫〕舻　〔聾〕聋　〔鷴〕鹇　〔戀〕恋

〔鷙〕鸷　〔鑄〕铸　〔襲〕龚　〔顯〕显　〔鷙〕鸷

〔霽〕霁　〔鑌〕镔　〔襲〕袭　〔蠱〕蛊　〔癰〕痈

【丨】　〔鑔〕镲　〔灘〕滩　〔髖〕髋　〔齋〕斋

〔齬〕龉　〔龕〕龛　〔灑〕洒　〔髕〕髌　〔罋〕罋

〔齦〕龈　〔糴〕籴　〔竊〕窃　【丿】　【一】

〔鱉〕鳖　〔鰳〕鳓　【フ】　〔籤〕签　〔鸂〕鸂

〔贖〕赎　〔鰹〕鲣　〔鷸〕鹬　〔讎〕雠　〔纓〕缨

〔躚〕跹　〔鰾〕鳔　〔彎〕彗　〔鷦〕鹪　〔纖〕纤

〔躓〕踬　〔鱈〕鳕　　　　　〔黴〕霉　〔纔〕才

〔蠨〕蟏　〔鰻〕鳗　**23 笔**　〔鑠〕铄　〔鷲〕鹫

〔囌〕苏　〔鱅〕鳙　【一】　〔鑕〕锧

〔囉〕罗　〔鰼〕鳛　〔瓚〕瓒　〔鑥〕镥　**24 笔**

〔囑〕嘱　〔玀〕猡　〔驛〕驿　〔鑣〕镳　【一】

〔輾〕辗　【丶】　〔驗〕验　〔鑞〕镴　〔鬢〕鬓

〔巔〕巅　〔讀〕读　〔攪〕搅　〔臢〕臜　〔攬〕揽

〔邐〕逦　　　　　〔欏〕椤　〔鱖〕鳜　〔驟〕骤

59

〔壩〕坝	〔鱠〕鲙	【丿】	【丨】	〔鑾〕銮
〔韆〕千	〔鱣〕鳣	〔籮〕箩	〔矚〕瞩	〔灩〕滟
〔觀〕观	【丶】	〔鑭〕镧	〔躪〕躏	【乛】
〔鹽〕盐	〔讕〕谰	〔鑰〕钥	〔躦〕躜	〔纜〕缆
〔釀〕酿	〔讖〕谶	〔鑲〕镶	【丿】	
〔黴〕霉	〔讒〕谗	〔饞〕馋	〔釁〕衅	**28 笔**
*〔靈〕灵	〔讓〕让	〔鱨〕鲿	〔鑷〕镊	
〔靄〕霭	〔鸛〕鹳	〔鱭〕鲚	〔鑹〕镩	〔鸛〕鹳
〔蠶〕蚕	〔鷹〕鹰	【丶】	【丶】	〔欞〕棂
【丨】	〔癱〕瘫	〔蠻〕蛮	〔灤〕滦	〔鑿〕凿
〔艷〕艳	〔癲〕癫	〔臠〕脔		〔鸚〕鹦
〔蘖〕蘖	〔贛〕赣	〔廳〕厅	**27 笔**	〔钁〕镢
〔齲〕龋	〔灝〕灏	〔灣〕湾		〔钁〕镢
〔齷〕龌	【乛】	【乛】	【一】	〔戀〕恋
〔鹼〕硷	〔鸝〕鹂	〔糶〕粜	〔鬮〕阄	
〔臟〕脏		〔纘〕缵	〔驤〕骧	**29 笔**
〔鷺〕鹭	**25 笔**		〔顳〕颞	
〔囑〕嘱		**26 笔**	【丨】	〔驪〕骊
〔羈〕羁	【一】		〔鸕〕鸬	〔鬱〕郁
【丿】	〔韉〕鞯	【一】	〔黷〕黩	
〔邁〕迈	〔欖〕榄	〔驥〕骥	【丿】	**30 笔**
〔籬〕篱	〔靉〕叆	〔驢〕驴	〔鑼〕锣	
〔籪〕簖	【丨】	〔趲〕趱	〔鑽〕钻	〔鸝〕鹂
〔黌〕黉	〔顱〕颅	〔顴〕颧	〔鱸〕鲈	〔饢〕馕
〔鱟〕鲎	〔躡〕蹑	〔黶〕黡	【丶】	〔鱺〕鲡
〔鱧〕鳢	〔躥〕蹿	〔釅〕酽	〔讞〕谳	〔鸞〕鸾
	〔鼉〕鼍		〔讜〕谠	**32 笔**
				〔籲〕吁